Issues in Contemporary Theology
Series Editor: I. Howard Marshall

The Origins of New Testament Christology
I. Howard Marshall

The Search for Salvation
David F. Wells

Christian Hope and the Future
Stephen H. Travis

Theology Encounters Revolution
J. Andrew Kirk

Theology Encounters Revolution

J. Andrew Kirk

InterVarsity Press
Downers Grove
Illinois 60515

Printed in America by InterVarsity Press, Downers Grove, Illinois, with permission from
Universities and Colleges Christian Fellowship, Leicester, England.

InterVarsity Press is the book-publishing division of Inter-Varsity Christian Fellowship,
a student movement active on campus at hundreds of universities, colleges
and schools of nursing. For information about local and regional activities, write
IVCF, 233 Langdon St., Madison, WI 53703.

Distributed in Canada through InterVarsity Press, 1875 Leslie St., Unit 10,
Don Mills, Ontario M3B 2M5, Canada.

ISBN 0-87784-468-2
Library of Congress Catalog Card Number: 80-7471

Printed in the United States of America

Library of Congress Cataloging in Publication Data
Kirk, J Andrew.
   Theology encounters revolution.

   (Issues in contemporary theology)
   Includes bibliographical references and index.
   1.   Revolution (Theology)–History of doctrines.
2.   Liberation theology.   I.   Title.   II.   Series.
BT738.3.K57   261.7   80-7471
ISBN 0-87784-468-2 (pbk.)

17	16	15	14	13	12	11	10	9	8	7	6	5	4	3	2	1
94	93	92	91	90	89	88	87	86	85	84	83	82	81	80		

62669

To the Kairos Community:
Carlos, Elsie, Mervin, Pedro, René, Samuel and Sidney, a group of the Lord's people committed to discovering fresh ways of serving the church in Latin America in the field of theological training and reflection.

The principal goal of education is to create men who are capable of doing new things, not simply of repeating what other generations have done — men who are creative, inventive, discoverers. The second goal of education is to form minds which can be critical, can verify, and not always accept everything they are offered.

Jean Piaget

Abbreviations

AACCB	*All African Conference of Churches Bulletin*
CC	*Christian Century*
CELAM	Consejo Episcopal Latinoamericano (Latin American Episcopal Council)
Conc.	*Concilium*
EQ	*Evangelical Quarterly*
ER	*Ecumenical Review*
ETR	*Etudes Théologiques et Religieuses*
Int.	*Interpretation*
LW	*Lutheran World*
PSB	*Princeton Seminary Bulletin*
RW	*Reformed World*
TT	*Theology Today*
USQR	*Union Seminary Quarterly Review*

Prologue

The fall of the Bastille on 14 July 1789 has cast its long shadow over all subsequent human history: princes and politicians, peasants and priests, professors of sociology and trade-union professionals, poets, novelists, students, communication experts and innumerable others, all have been either fascinated, drawn, repelled or inspired by this singular event. By the mid-1950s the shadow had reached even the ivory towers of professional theologians.

Ten years later 'theologies of revolution' had become a boom subject and an extremely marketable commodity. By the mid-1970s interest in the social and political implications of theological thought continued unabated. Today the relationship between theology and revolution still seems to be high on the agenda of contemporary Christian thinking.

In this book we shall attempt to describe the rise of this interest and the varied forms it has taken in different parts of the world church. A tentative exploration will also be made of the biblical and theological foundations of revolution, to ask whether, in fact, a theology of revolution is a viable proposition at all.

The subject-matter of our study, therefore, divides quite naturally into three parts. The first part is general and historical, and we start by trying to understand the often highly charged and ambiguous word 'revolution' through an examination of the historical development (chapter 1) and the contemporary significance (chapter 2) of its meaning. At the same time it is important to realize that the precise way of doing theology is now a matter of intense and lively debate. Many persistent assumptions, springing from a different age and mentality, are now being seriously questioned. New approaches to the subject have arisen, particularly in the younger churches of the Third World, largely as a response to the challenge of revolution in the post-war period. In chapter 3, therefore, we look at some of the most important forerunners of contemporary revolutionary theology.

The second part of the book presents a review of the ideas of some of the principal exponents of a revolutionary theology. The order of the chapters is not especially important; it follows the geographical pattern in which theological institutions were founded and spread. Perhaps for this reason it describes an increasing radicalization of both the content and method of theological reflection on revolution.

The final section of the book attempts to evaluate the impact of revolution on theological thinking. I believe that this task can be carried out adequately only if we are prepared to allow the Scriptures to be the *norma normans* of all genuinely *Christian* thought. Such a stance means that each Christian must be willing to accept the judgment of the text both on his formulations of belief and on his ethical decisions.

Unfortunately, experience has proved that our acceptance of the full critical and creative authority of God's Word in its written form is no guarantee that we hear its message aright. All kinds of prejudices, fears of change and ignorance, whether wilful or otherwise, continually frustrate a really honest and obedient hearing of the gospel message. Particularly important in this respect are the many unexamined assumptions which stem from our social and cultural backgrounds. They tend to bias our understanding of the Scriptures in a number of different directions.

This means that alongside our acceptance of the full authority of the Bible we also need a thoroughgoing and constant enquiry into the relationship between man's personal and social environment and his interpretation of the biblical text. I am increasingly convinced that the full authority of Scripture over the lives of Christian people can be effective only as and when we find a fresh approach to its interpretation which will provide an alternative both to orthodox critical scholarship and to the traditional evangelical, 'confessional' hermeneutic.

The impact of revolution has demonstrated that the way both groups interpret the Bible is no longer adequate for the church's task in the modern world. Critical scholarship, for example, often seems to ignore the importance of our being able to hear what message the text has for us today. It engages in a minutely detailed study of particular passages, concentrating more on the origin and transmission of the texts than on their impact in their final written form. Contemporary exegetical studies, therefore, treat the text as if it were a pure object, ready to reveal its meaning to those who apply the right scholarly techniques. The great mistake inherent in this method, I believe, is to assume that we can really understand Scripture by debating its meaning purely on the level of ideas and concepts. The Bible simply cannot be treated as if it were any kind of ancient literature. In the face of its demand to be considered as a subject which questions and challenges the reader to decide for or against its message, a purely objective approach is far from being neutral and scientific. If, then, we are to find a comprehensively biblical approach to revolution, we need firstly to analyse our willingness or refusal to accept the Bible's message at its face value, and also to examine our political and social attitudes and commitments; only then may we employ the really valuable technical tools of exegesis.

The problem with much evangelical interpretation of Scripture is that it allows pre-packaged doctrinal confessions to dictate the way in which Scripture is to be understood. Whereas such confessions may play a legitimate role in marking out certain genuine limits to interpretation, too often they are brakes on serious enquiry. There is a danger that the very constraints they impose may outweigh their positive role, especially if we forget that these confessions are historically and culturally conditioned and are never completely and finally coterminous with the biblical message itself. In some churches and para-church organizations, loyalty to a particular confession, formulation or tradition has become a serious substitute for creative study and application of the Scriptures. This has usually led to an inflexible attitude which excludes new challenges, such as that posed by revolution. Here also, though in a different way, the text is treated as a purely objective entity, a quarry for arguments to defend doctrines, theories and practices. Yet those very doctrines, theories and practices need to be regularly tested, and this can be done only if we are always open to receive new insights into the Bible's meaning for today.

In the case of both critical scholarship and the evangelical 'confessional' hermeneutic, interpretation is made to depend largely on

11

criteria drawn from outside the biblical message itself. By being given a certain autonomy these criteria act as a kind of canon outside the Canon; whereas, in order to arrive at a faithful understanding of the Bible's meaning, we must allow the biblical message to speak to us on its own terms. A proper inductive approach to the text will begin, then, with a study of the Bible from its own point of view. Because of the way in which we so easily remain oblivious to our own historically conditioned points of view, biblical interpretation must be seen as a constant struggle to allow the message of Scripture to be independent of our multiple biases. The full authority of Scripture can be exercised only when it is set free to be a critical instrument in the life of the church. We might speak here of a truly 'prophetic hermeneutic'.

Because the proper relationship between theology and revolution can be settled only by an adequate biblical hermeneutic, we shall return again to this question in the chapter on the biblical material, not engaging in a theoretical debate about hermeneutics (which is not the subject-matter of this book), but trying to show in outline how one may use the Bible hermeneutically. Hermeneutics as I understand it is the task of transposing the biblical message from one situation to another: an attempt to understand how the Word of God, which was written and lived out some 2,000 or more years ago, can command obedience in today's contexts. We hope that some of the ideas suggested there may help to carry forward the debate about revolution and theology. The reader will be able to judge the extent to which the method used points the way forward to a more meaningful use of Scripture in relation to the pressing challenges of this revolutionary, turbulent world.

A book on revolution cannot ignore the complex problem of violence. It has almost always accompanied social change, even when exercised by individuals or small groups. Such a complex and polemical subject demands a systematic, continuous treatment of its own. To do this in a short study like ours is ambitious and risky, but we felt it was worth attempting, even if no very definite conclusions have been reached.

This brief outline of its contents may appear to promise more than the book can fulfil. I am deeply conscious of its limitations, and in order to save my critics time I shall mention some of them now.

As revolutionary theology has been a boom subject for a number of years, it has been beyond my resources to study 'all the relevant literature', as the pundits love to put it. My detailed knowledge of some areas is limited, particularly of North America. I believe I have selected the most representative, or formative, of both coloured and white writers. I have also tried to understand and to be fair to what I have read. This is a difficult task because personal prejudices and blindnesses so easily distort one's understanding of another's thought. If my evaluation is at times superficial, others, reacting against it, may be able to clarify issues I have missed. In that event, this study will at least have served as a goad to produce a more excellent result. We must never allow ourselves to be trapped into thinking that the discussion is closed, that there exists some final, authoritative and orthodox statement about a Christian's response to revolution. At this moment we can probably attempt little more than an excursion from areas where our Christian commitment is clear and beyond question into areas where many ambiguities still abound. I hope that in the discussion which follows I may help the unwary by clearing some of the obstacles away from the path which leads from one to the other.

The greatest problem in attempting to do justice to this vast and controversial subject is not so much temporal (lack of time for devouring extensive bibliographies) as spatial (the lack of opportunity for geographical identification). Every revolutionary theology has emerged from the challenge of a particular historical situation, so that for those at a distance real understanding is difficult. At the same time, proximity does not guarantee that the issues involved will be clearly grasped. We can console ourselves with the thought that few people, if any, have had the opportunity of living for a long period in all the areas under review. Few, therefore, have been personally involved in all of the movements, changes, activities and stirrings of conscience which in the last two decades have provoked Christian thinkers to write about revolution.

My basic aim, then, is to provide a limited survey of a vast terrain, introducing the reader to the most important landmarks and explaining to him the most significant features. It is a guide to the debate about theology and revolution, and although basically it tries to explain the map as it now exists, at times it risks suggestions as to how the cartography might be improved. My hope is that the reader will be stimulated to lay aside the use of another's compass and set about mapping new territory for himself.

Andrew Kirk

PART I

Revolution? Theology?
Revolutionary theology?

Chapter One

Revolution behind the scenes

Louis XVI on hearing of the fall of the Bastille exclaimed, 'C'est une révolte'; and Liancourt corrected him: 'Non, sire, c'est une révolution.'

Hannah Arendt, *On Revolution* (1963).

Understanding a slogan

Those who are aware of the power of modern propaganda and its tendency to distort reality will understand why the term 'revolution' has become so debased in modern usage. In Latin America almost every change in government is called a revolution. Many political parties use the word 'revolutionary' in their title, even when their respective aims are obviously contradictory.

Apparently the term is still a political asset, even when many people are highly sceptical about the political pretence which lies behind it. The power of suggestion hidden in the word, and communicated through connotation and association rather than through content and analysis, make it hard to grasp its real significance.

The task is further complicated by the changes in meaning through which the word has passed in the course of a few centuries. Originally it was used in astronomy in the late Middle Ages to describe the apparently fixed revolving motion of the stars: a recurring, cyclical movement quite beyond man's influence. In this sense it aptly conveyed the fatalistic outlook of those who first used it to describe the violent changes of government – the 'rivoluzioni' – which quickly followed one another in the city states of Renaissance Italy.

The concepts of return, recurrence and inevitability have remained with the word even in its later, more explicitly political usage from the 17th century onwards. Lord Clarendon calls the overthrow of the Protectorate and the *restoration* of the monarchy a 'revolution'.

Tom Paine in his book *The Rights of Man* calls the American and French revolutions 'renovations of the natural order of things.'

This emphasis on the restoration of an ideal past finds its modern counterpart in the military *coups* of Latin America. What must be restored is the mythical ideal of a unified society, based on long-standing 'Christian' and 'Western' traditions, which is threatened either by party conflict or guerrilla activity.

Even the cataclysmic events of the French revolution, though apparently promising vast changes and renewal, were really based on the motivating power of a primitive ideal: the belief, propounded by Rousseau, in man's original goodness in a state of nature.

However, the idea of return implicit in a cyclical view of time has, at least in theory, been strongly supplanted by that of change, innovation and progress. The *novus ordo* is possible only on the basis of rectilinear time.

The use of the word 'revolution' in the modern scientific sphere should help us gain a greater understanding of its meaning. Such terms as technological, cybernetic or ecological revolution make it clear that some kind of qualitative change is meant, and the same is true of production or managerial revolutions in the economic or business fields. They describe the physical transformation of a situation in such a way as to make a return to the previous situation – often described as primitive – either unthinkable or clearly impossible.

When this meaning is applied to the political realm it expressly contradicts all ideas of restoration and repetition. The change in the political meaning of the word parallels the rise of the modern sciences towards the end of the 18th century.

Revolution, then, denotes changing one kind of political and social order for another. It implies the destruction of one system and its replacement by another, for which there is no exact working model in past history.

Political revolution has become closely identified today with certain 'messianic' ideologies, some variant of Marxism clearly being the most influential. But there are other ideologies or world-views, such as National Socialism or Islam, which have also provoked profound political changes. The attempt to understand the meaning of revolution in any particular context should not be confused with value judgments concerning the legitimacy of any particular revolution.

No one definition of revolution could possibly achieve universal acceptance. For the purpose of this study I shall adopt one that I have already used elsewhere: 'revolution is the arrival of a qualitatively new factor in human history which radically changes the future direction of a people who already possess a long tradition from the past.'[1]

This meaning may then be amplified according to a particular ideological stance. If one is a Marxist, 'the classical definition is that of transference of power from one class to another. A social revolution is made when one class expropriates the properties of another and nationalizes them. A political revolution is made when the political power of one class is expropriated and another takes it in its hands. Such a political revolution may be achieved by an army uprising which topples one government and places in power revolutionary representatives.'[2] If one espouses the cause of National Socialism, revolution will involve the overthrow of modern democracy and the capitalist system in an attempt to build a unified society of qualitatively new men based on the values of folk-nationalism, self-denial, the unification of intellectual and manual labour, discipline and the will to conquer.[3]

So far our discussion of definitions has been theoretical, so in order to test and expand our understanding of the contemporary use of the word we shall now survey various stages of the growth of revolutionary consciousness. We should remember, however, that the reality of revolution covers more ground than we can possibly deal with here. It is related to such concepts as messianism, millennium, utopia, ideology, power, violence and class struggle.

Revolution from the Middle Ages to the 20th century

Utopian expectations up to the Reformation
Belief in the possibilities of a new earthly existence radically different from the prevailing structures of feudal Europe sprang to life in the

---

[1] J. A. Kirk, *Jesucristo revolucionario* (Buenos Aires, 1974), p. 15.
[2] Isaac Deutscher, *On the Chinese Cultural Revolution* (London, 1966).
[3] *Cf.* J. Ellul, *De la révolution aux révoltes* (Paris, 1972), pp. 209–219.

late Middle Ages. It was fostered by a determined resistance to the prevailing institutions of the day, especially to the church which had by then gained for itself enormous secular privileges. It also marked an incipient social unrest and, as in the case of the English Peasants' Revolt, an awareness of the possibilities of social change. Concerning this uprising of 1381 Michael Hill makes some important observations:

> The political objectives of this revolt are set against the background of a labour shortage after the Black Death, as a result of which the peasants saw an opportunity for demanding that manorial dues be commuted for cash rents and villeinage be replaced by wage labour. However, to the rebel gathering at Blackheath, John Ball preached a much more radical set of demands . . . (He) argued in favour of an ideal of equality based on the notion of a Golden Age at the beginning of creation when all men had been created free and equal . . . When the evil nobles had been destroyed, he prophesied, the millennium in which all men would live in an egalitarian State of Nature would be ushered in.[4]

At times utopian expectations grew directly from the deep stirrings of nationalism. Such was the case of the rebellion in Bohemia which followed the burning of John Huss in 1415 and of his disciple, Jerome of Prague, in the following year.

The Taborites, one of the parties opposed to the Holy Roman Emperor Sigismund and to the decrees of the Council of Constance (1414), withdrew to a hill which they renamed Mount Tabor (according to a tradition that this would be the place of Christ's return). Their beliefs contained many utopian features, such as the possession of all goods in common. As the group came under physical pressure it switched from a pacifist stance to aggression. It embarked on a crusade whose aim was to sweep away a corrupt and heretical church and the whole apparatus of a privileged society. Only then could a Golden Age of equality return, in which taxes, rents and private property would exist no longer.[5] The group disappeared soon after being defeated in 1434 by its former allies, the Utraquists, who had

---

[4] M. Hill, *A Sociology of Religion* (London, 1973), pp. 208–209.
[5] *Ibid.*, p. 209.

meanwhile forged some kind of compromise with the Catholic Church.

As might be expected, the great majority of utopian movements of this period started as protest movements against the religious establishment. Inspiration for a wholly new order came from the apocalyptic strains of early Christianity, seemingly suppressed when the church, after Constantine, became the official organizer of the state's religious life.[6] This was almost the only possible basis from which to protest against the sacrilege of identifying the institutions of church and empire with God's eternal order, and to search for a new order.

It is a moot question whether these movements reflected a genuine social protest against existing conditions, or simply a religious escapism into what Cohn calls 'salvationist fantasies'.[7] The answer will depend largely on whether or not one accepts a consistently materialist interpretation of history. We shall return to this question later, but for the moment we turn to two aspects of the examples given above which are particularly relevant to our discussion. Firstly, a 'reforming' and a 'revolutionary' stream are apparent in each case; the one desiring significant but limited changes in a basically immovable order, the other demanding the replacement of the old order by something qualitatively different. Secondly, the movements were made up almost wholly of the lower social groups, though sometimes their leaders were educated men.[8] These and other revolutionary movements reflect the beginning of a serious questioning of the idea that the given structure of societies was an unalterable fact of the universe. The 16th-century political and religious challenge to the unity of the West took this questioning a step further.

Radical movements in the Reformation and beyond

Both reform and revolution were championed by the various movements which initiated and consolidated the Protestant opposition to the undivided church in the West.

---

[6] The late Middle Ages was a period of considerable religious protest and renewal, as witness the rapid spread of the Waldenses, the Lollards, the Hussites, the mystical movements of Meister Eckhart and John Tauler, and the Brethren of the Common Life.

[7] Cf. The Pursuit of the Millennium (London, 1970).

[8] Cf. Peter Worsley, The Trumpet shall Sound (London, 1968), p. 68.

Though they were united in their profound rejection of Roman Catholic theology and institutions, there were significant differences of opinion between the 'mainstream' and 'radical' parties of the Reformation concerning the social meaning of the Christian faith.

These differences first came to a head during the Peasant War in Germany of 1524–5. In March 1525 the insurrectionists put forward twelve articles demanding the redress of serious social injustices: *e.g.* the abolishment of small tithes and serfdom, the proper payment of labour, the fixing of just rents, the restoration of common lands and the use of forests given to the poor.

They were inspired to press their demands, if necessary by revolutionary war, by the apocalyptic preaching of Thomas Müntzer. Drawing on biblical texts, he specifically denounced the right of private property and rejected all class distinctions. He was a revolutionary in the strict sense of the word, looking for the implementation of a totally new order in Germany based on the creation of a new 'spiritual' community.

Luther, though at first sympathetic to the peasants' grievances, rejected both Müntzer's theological extremism and his willingness to carry the peasants' cause to armed conflict.

How we interpret Luther's denunciation of 'the murderous and thieving rabble of peasants' will depend largely on our particular theological and ideological standpoint. Luther's defenders argue that his opposition came only when the rebel movement had turned anarchist in theory and practice; that, because the German princes were unlikely to adopt programmes of radical reform, he was forced to view change as a long-term process; and that, finally, his defence of order against violent revolution was based upon the Christian's calling to submit to the governing authorities. Luther's critics point out that there is an obvious contradiction between his political expediency and his religious intransigence; that his interpretation of the Scriptures was partial, thus denying his own principle of *sola scriptura*; and, finally, that his support for the suppression of the peasants and his subsequent distrust of the common man simply reflect his own class background.

There is clearly some truth in both interpretations. They depend very largely on the suppositions which guide them and they exemplify two divergent approaches which Christians tend to make to social problems.

In the 16th century the two approaches produced a sharp disagreement over proper church/state relations. This was felt particularly acutely in Zwingli's Zürich. The rise of the Anabaptist movement displayed both theological and political concerns. They rejected infant baptism because they believed that there was no warrant for it in the New Testament. But their stance also implied a rejection of religious uniformity as a guarantee of the orderly continuance of the state, a belief inherited by the principal reformers from the Constantine tradition of the unity of church and empire.[9] The Anabaptists were, thus, in a real sense the first non-conformists and the first advocates in the modern era of a pluralist and open society.

The movement arose as the result of a strong charismatic leadership, and developed as separate communities in different lands. Some, like John of Leiden who led the group in Münster (1533-35), and Melchior Hoffmann, a leader in Strasbourg until his imprisonment in 1533, believed that they were God's special instruments for the inauguration of a new world order. Others, like Balthasar Hübmaier and Menno Simons, believed that Christian communities should be organized separately from the state, should refuse military service, but should not directly seek to overthrow existing society. At first sight, the former represent revolution in that they espoused a complete break between all previous societies and the new Jerusalem that they promised to set up. A more profound analysis of revolution, however, may well lead us to view the latter group as more revolutionary. In any case, modern debate about revolution continues to circle round many of the same issues which divided the Anabaptists from each other and from mainstream Protestantism and Roman Catholicism.

One hundred years later in Puritan England certain millenarian views briefly sparked to life again round the Fifth Monarchy Men, the Levellers and the Diggers:

The 'levellers' demanded . . . natural rights and political equality for all

---

[9] At the Diet of Augsburg (1530) the Protestant German Estates proclaimed a law banishing ecclesiastical dissidents from Protestant territories, while the Catholic Diet of Speier (1528) invoked against them the old Roman law against heretics.

men. The 'diggers' went further, wanting to restore economic equality, and they tried to abolish private property and establish agrarian communities reestablishing the original communism of the state of nature and terminating the feudal slavery of the English peasants. The Fifth Monarchy Men united all these hopes of a restored paradise in the expectation of an imminent coming of the victorious Christ, the defender of the poor, who would straighten out all social, political and ecclesiastical evils, and establish God's direct rule over the Earth.[10]

The dawn of modern revolution in the Age of Reason

Belief in a coming new world order of righteousness and equality through God's transcendental action gave place at the beginning of the 18th century to a belief that man was intrinsically capable of effecting this radical change himself. The theoretical base for this dramatic change of outlook was Deism.

Deism arose as an alternative to orthodox theism at the end of the 17th century with the publication of John Toland's book *Christianity not Mysterious* (1696). It reached its final, classical and virulently anti-Christian expression in Thomas Paine's passionate work *Age of Reason* (1794–6). As a new mode of philosophical thinking it initially reflected the pragmatic and latitudinarian reaction of the British to the millenarian excesses of the 17th century. Part of its intention, undoubtedly, was to arrest the messianic fanaticism which was based on the claim to immediate divine illumination uncontrolled by free, rational reflection. The reality of God, his authority over and purpose for the world and his continuing action within it, were banished to the very edge of existence. From now on man, aided by the pseudo-illumination given by the study of nature, became the measure of the right and the good.

In British economic and political thinking, Deism provided the impulse for the growth of liberalism, whose father was John Locke. Locke proclaimed reasonableness in the approach to Christianity, and pluralism and toleration in the political sphere.

However, by a curious twist of history, those, like Voltaire, Rousseau and the Encyclopaedists, who were particularly influential in

---

[10] R. Radford Ruether, *The Political Kindgom: the Western Experience of Messianic Hope* (New York, 1970).

the surge of revolutionary fervour in France which finally ended the *Ancien Régime*, also imbibed Deism. It became a sharp, intellectual weapon with which to ridicule the absolutist pretensions of the church to be the only mediator of divine authority and the upholder of the only legitimate divine order on earth, namely the monarchy.[11] The revolutionaries brutally challenged the supernatural sanction given to the rigid division of society into rulers and ruled, each of whom, by reason of birth, held an immutable place in the world.

The fact that Deism marked the beginning of a new faith was perhaps more significant for the world than its critical stance. Linked to the rise of modern science (which was arguably the most momentous event of the 17th century), Deism was imbued with an empiricist view of reality. The proper object of man's reasoning was no longer philosophical speculation but the natural world. David Hume replaced Descartes as the philosopher of the new age.

The new faith was extremely optimistic about man's ability to build a new world. The old philosophical speculation was allied with religious superstition, but, by ridding humanity of both, man's innate possibilities would shine forth. Man would no longer be guided by obsolete religious ideals and moral absolutes but by the light of natural reason reflecting the reality of the given world.

The classic expression of belief in the arrival of a new beginning to humanity is Condorcet's *Esquisse d'un Tableau historique des Progrès de l'Esprit humain* (1793). In this work he describes how universal education will be the instrument used to make mankind aware that social divisions and privileges are evil and to achieve a new society giving equal opportunities to all.

Unfortunately, education was not an adequate tool for the creation of a revolutionary society. The new kingdom of man was seized by violence, and violent men became its first citizens. However, the violence which initiated the revolution did not compare with the violence which sustained it. At the beginning moderates came to power, among them Robespierre. They were men with high liberal ideals who believed that mankind was capable of unselfish action,

---

[11] The passionately anti-ecclesiastical nature of revolution was also apparent in the Latin American Wars of Independence (1810–24), though here, as in France, the lower order of the clergy often actively supported the revolutionary cause.

solidarity and justice, once the structures of exploitation had been dismantled.[12]

The French Revolution, however, took a more radical path. By the middle of 1793 the moderates were defeated and the notorious Terror began. Robespierre, who underwent a strange transformation,[13] was its instigator.

The reign of terror had a more subtle cause than the natural spiralling effect of violence. It filled the void created by the application of philosophical innocence to hard political reality. The new view of man in nature demanded a new type of society where virtue, logically, would reign. So the Jacobin party under Robespierre castigated the lack of virtue as hypocrisy, every element of which, real or imagined, it hunted down and purged. However, the unmasking of hypocrisy did not lead to freedom, but to rage, despair and finally doom. Robespierre fell in 1794. On the 18th Brumaire in the new revolutionary calendar (*i.e.* October 1799) Napoleon made his *coup d'état*. By 1814 the Bourbons were restored.

History in France seemed to have moved through a complete cycle: revolution gave place first to reaction and then to restoration. Revolutionary change seemed to have followed the fixed order of the stars. The state passed from monarchy to democracy, to anarchy, tyranny and back to monarchy. 'Such is the circle', had commented Machiavelli, 'through which all republics are destined to run.' All, that is, except the newly constituted United States of America.

Can the American Revolution of 1776 really be classified as such? Hannah Arendt thinks it can. True, it has hardly inspired subsequent revolutionary movements as has the French Revolution, but it qualifies because if fulfils an essential condition of all true revolutions: the founding of a newly ordered society. Nevertheless, like the French Revolution, it also failed to maintain its revolutionary momentum, not because the new values failed to fill the vacuum left by the overthrow of the old, but because the accelerated rise in prosperity converted the quest for freedom, with every citizen 'a genuine participator in the government of affairs' (Jefferson), into

---

[12] *Cf.* Crane Brinton, *The Anatomy of Revolution* (New York, 1952²), pp. 155–156.

[13] Hannah Arendt, *On Revolution* (New York, 1963), pp. 70–110, brilliantly describes the inevitable fulfilment of Vergniaud's famous *bon mot:* 'the revolution, like Saturn, devours its children.'

the quest for private welfare.[14] Miss Arendt believes that the American Revolution is the only one which had even a slender chance of prolonging its revolutionary vigour. Because it adopted a realistic rather than a sentimental view of human nature, it advocated civil law rather than boundless violence as a means of transforming one regime into another. Moreover, it did not have to solve the 'social question', the problem of widespread and acute human misery.

Nevertheless, the revolutionary initiative was thwarted and the vision was betrayed:

> Freedom was reinterpreted as free-enterprise . . . (which is) a minor blessing in comparison with true political freedom – speech and thought, assembly and association. . . . What was lost in the USA was the revolutionary spirit. What was left was: civil liberties, individual welfare of the greatest number, public opinion in a democratic society.[15]

In other words revolution evolved into liberalism; and liberalism, according to the most rigorous revolutionary tradition, is the quintessence of counterfeit change.

The inevitability of revolution
Revolution needed an interpreter who could give clear reasons for its previous failures and a basis for its conversion into something of permanent value. Such a person was Karl Marx, undoubtedly the most influential thinker of the 19th century.

Marx was initially indebted to the French revolutionary tradition. In the years between 1838 and 1843 he tried to discover the reasons why the French Revolution, though seemingly so progressive, had failed to produce the equal, free and brotherly society which it had promised. His conclusions demonstrate the radical nature of his historical analysis and mark a significant rupture with all previous revolutionary thinking.

The theoretical basis for the rupture is found in his materialistic explanation of the development of society: society changes according to the changes in its economic base. Armed with this general theory, Marx debunked all views of history which make man's ideas the

[14] *Ibid.*, pp. 112–137.   [15] *Ibid.*, pp. 219, 223.

main catalyst of change (*i.e.* idealism). For Brunno Bauer, an erst-while colleague of Marx and like him one of the Young Hegelians, the French Revolution had been driven along by the lofty ideas of the intellectual élite. These ideas, however, were betrayed by the passion and ignorance of the masses, and so the revolution failed. Marx believed that it had nevertheless achieved something positive:

> Camille Desmoulins, Danton, Robespierre, Saint-Just, Napoleon, the heroes, as well as the parties and the masses of the old French Revolution performed the task *of their time* . . . of releasing and setting up modern bourgeois society. The first ones knocked the feudal basis to pieces and mowed off the feudal heads which had grown from it. The other created inside France the conditions under which free competition could first be developed. . . .[16]

The direction of Marx's break with the revolutionary thinking of his time can be clearly seen from this quotation. His belief that the economic forces of production were the underlying, driving power of all human history led him to adopt a semi-deterministic view of the development of society. Revolutionary progress could only be achieved when the material conditions of society were ripe for it. Thus the leaders of the French Revolution 'performed the task of their time.' They swept away feudal society and created bourgeois society to take its place.

This was, for Marx, a revolutionary act because the development of productive forces demanded that it should happen in this way. Nevertheless, its revolutionary implication was quite insignificant in comparison with the Industrial Revolution, a unique combination of new scientific inventions and the liberal forces of the new bourgeois class:

> Steam, electricity and the self-acting mule were revolutionists of a rather more dangerous character than even citizens Barbès, Raspail and Blanqui (a reference to the leaders of the 1848 revolution).[17]

The Industrial Revolution, in its turn, gave birth to the proletariat.

---

[16] *The Eighteenth Brumaire of Louis Bonaparte* (1852) in R. C. Tucker (ed.), *Marx-Engels Reader* (New York, 1972), p. 427 (my italics).
[17] *Speech at the Anniversary of the People's Paper* (1856), in *ibid.*, p. 427.

This new class, like the bourgeois class of 18th century France and America, would forge a new and total revolution in existing society:

> The working men . . . are as much the invention of modern time as machinery itself. . . . They will then, certainly, not be the last in aiding the social revolution produced by that industry, a revolution, which means the emancipation of their own class all over the world, which is as universal as capital-rule and wages-slavery.[18]

Marx's view of revolution is new because he has produced a theory to explain the failure of past revolutions – they could not, historically, be more than partial realizations of a total emancipation – and he has demonstrated why the coming revolution would be total and permanent.

The cornerstone of the theory is his analysis of human alienation. Basically, man is alienated because of his relationship to the means of production. This relationship is determined, in Marx's thinking, by his theory of value:

> The value of labouring power is determined by the value of the necessities required to produce, develop, maintain and perpetuate labour power (*i.e.* a physically fit worker). Over and above the values of these necessities and the cost of raw materials, the capitalist has acquired a profit which is converted into an accumulation of capital and used as *surplus-value*. This surplus-value gives the capitalist the ability to buy and use *labouring-power* in the same way as manufactured goods on the basis of supply and demand, the law of the so-called 'free enterprise' system.[19]

The worker's alienation from his work is the natural and inevitable result of the capitalist system. Its counterpart, among the owners of capital, is exploitation.

Marx believed that this situation had to end because capitalism, like feudalism, had produced forces which would result in its own inevitable dissolution. Capitalism, because of its own success, would eventually collapse through a crisis of over-production. The working class, meanwhile, having become an increasingly organized group in

---

[18] *Ibid.*, p. 428.   [19] *Cf. Wage Labour and Capital* (1849) in *ibid.*, pp. 167–190.

order to defend their own interests, would take over society for their own benefit. Their first task would be

> to wrest, by degrees, all capital from the bourgeoisie, centralize all instruments of production in the hands of the State and increase the total of productive forces as rapidly as possible.[20]

This transitional period between a capitalist and a communist society may be called socialism. It envisages the 'revolutionary dictatorship of the proletariat.' When a fully-fledged communist society was created there would be no more division of labour nor private property:

> The social anarchy of production gives place to a social regulation of production upon a definite plan according to the needs of the community and each individual.[21]

Marx never predicted the exact time or nature of the revolution, though he indicated some of the conditions necessary for its arrival. He believed, however, that it was as inevitable as the scientific progress of man. When it came mankind would, at last, be created anew for a new life of communal solidarity, creativity and abundance.[22]

Revolution: booms and recessions

If the 19th century saw the development of a coherent and persuasive theory of revolution,[23] the 20th century has seen various attempts at making it a permanent reality.

The first, and most important, was carried through by Lenin and the Bolshevik party. It implied a revolution within the revolution.

---

[20] *The Communist Manifesto* (1848) in *ibid.*, p. 352.

[21] Engels, *Socialism: Utopian and Scientific* (1880) in *ibid.*, p. 634.

[22] Further on the subject see D. McLellan, *The Thought of Karl Marx: an Introduction* (London, 1971), Part II, chapters 7 and 8; R. Tucker, *The Marxian Revolutionary Idea* (London, 1970).

[23] Let it not be forgotten that there were many other revolutionary theorists of the 19th century whom space does not permit us to include. Many of them crossed swords with Marx. Their views were not always less relevant, but certainly they have been a lot less influential. *Cf.* G. D. H. Cole, *A History of Socialist Thought*, Vol. II (London, 1954); G. Lichtheim, *The Origins of Socialism* (New York, 1968).

Marx, and later Plekhanov in Russia, believed that the proletariat's rise to power and the ending of strife between classes are consequences of the full development of capitalist society. Marx had in mind the nations of Western Europe, already in an advanced stage of industrialization. The conditions for the socialist revolution of which he spoke were not present in feudal Russia. Social relationships in Russia in 1889 were similar to those which had existed a hundred years earlier in France on the eve of the Revolution and the objective conditions for the establishment of socialism there seemed to be at least another hundred years away.

However, Marx was not altogether consistent in his views on revolution. In 1872 he stated that the working class might achieve power by constitutional means and then legally change the constitution to expropriate the capitalist class.[24] In 1875 and 1882 he stated that a transition to socialism was possible, after all, in a society like Russia, even though it did not possess an authentic proletarian class.[25] In fact Marx simply resorted to guess-work concerning the outbreak of revolution. Subsequent history has proved him essentially inaccurate. Lenin cannot be blamed, therefore, if he developed one aspect of the Marxist revolutionary tradition into a new theory of revolution. He chose the Blanquist model of the control of popular movements by an élite of 'professional revolutionaries'.[26] He justifies his transformation of Marx's thinking in the following paragraph:

> The history of all countries shows that the working class exclusively by its own effort, is able to develop only trade-union consciousness. . . . The theory of socialism, however, grew out of the philosophic, historical and economic theories that were elaborated by the educated representatives of the propertied classes, the intellectuals. . . . In the very same way, in Russia, the theoretical doctrine of social-democracy arose quite independently of the spontaneous growth of the working-class movement; it arose as a natural and inevitable outcome of the development of ideas among the revolutionary socialist intelligentsia.[27]

[24] *Speech at Amsterdam* (1872).
[25] *Marx on Bakunin* (1875); *Preface to the Russian Edition of the Communist Manifesto* (1882).
[26] *Cf.* G. Lichtheim, *Marxism: an Historical and Critical Study* (London, 1964), p. 128.
[27] Quoted in A. P. Mendel (ed.), *Essential Works of Marxism* (New York, 1961), p. 93.

Lenin, by promising revolution in Russia through a tightly knit, disciplined party allied to the proletariat, but directing them from above, made a radical theoretical split with the elaboration by Marx of economic factors in the evolution of capitalism into socialism. That this was a serious departure from Marx can be seen by studying Engels' reply to an open letter by the Russian populist leader Pyotr Tkachev, *On Social Relations in Russia* (1875).[28] Though Engels believed that Russia was 'undoubtedly on the eve of a revolution', he denied that it could be achieved prematurely by what he contemptuously described as the Bakunist, anarchist model of direct armed conflict.

Lenin achieved power in October 1917 because the incompetent and vacillating provisional government, which had failed to solve either the problem of Russia's involvement in the war or the peasants' demand for land, provided him with a fleeting opportunity. In fact, the October Revolution was no real revolution, nor even a *coup d'état*, for it met with almost no resistance. It signified the provision of an organized, ideologically articulate power-structure of government where one no longer existed. The Bolsheviks came to power because no one else could govern.[29] The Leninist model of revolution, however,

> amounted to the political expropriation of the proletariat and its subjection to a dictatorial machine operated by the Bolshevik leadership: a leadership which was essentially self-constituted and irremovable.[30]

This model has had far-reaching consequences. It is based on the élitist control of the working class through a centralized bureaucratic state machinery. In almost every way, with the exception of the formal socializing of the means of production, it has proved the very antithesis of Marx's own prediction of a new society. The model has been adopted by every subsequent Marxist-inspired revolution, particularly those of China (1949) and Cuba (1959), and by would-be revolutionary guerrillas all over the world. Before a new order can be built the reins of power must be seized.

[28] *Marx-Engels Reader*, pp. 589–599.
[29] Cf. N. F. Cantor, *The Age of Protest: Dissent and Rebellion in the Twentieth Century* (London, 1970), pp. 60–84. [30] G. Lichtheim, *Marxism*, p. 337.

At the same time, certain Marxist parties of the West have for tactical and other reasons practically abandoned the model. Returning to Marx's own theoretical base, they are trying to recognize the objective historical conditions for revolution today. Their task is hampered by two important factors. Firstly, Marxism has developed in a rigid and dogmatic way into a fossilized creed, rather than remaining an adaptable political and economic tool of analysis. Secondly, radical changes in the development of capitalism and political institutions in the West and the advent of a Third World consciousness have profoundly changed the context of revolution since Marx's day.

Within the last two decades revolution has come to mean many different things: among others, existential protest, changes in art forms and means of communication; Black Power; nationalistic aspirations; the heightening of inner consciousness and the philosophical use of drugs.

The revolutionary scene today is vast, varied and volatile.[31] Much of it, even when overtly dedicated to purely political and social ends, contains an important element of personal search for identity and meaning. Though we have basically limited ourselves to discussing the social meaning of revolution, for this is the background against which revolutionary theologies have developed, the personal context and aspirations of revolutionaries cannot be ignored without gravely simplifying the issues.

---

[31] Ellul's book (see note 3) is one of the most complete discussions of recent manifestations of revolution. His basic thesis is that there is actually only one revolutionary force operating in the modern world: technology. In this sense he may be closer to Marx than the modern revolutionary, whose struggle for power is more akin to a utopic revolt, a reaction to an almost irresistible power. However, modern technology, far from sowing the seeds for the destruction of the bourgeois class, has tightened their control on power.

33

Chapter Two

Revolution takes its cue

Ours is an age of romantic revolutionaries performing romantic acts.
Eric Hobsbawm, *The Listener* (1972).

The revolutionary will of both individuals and groups is fed on utopian expectations. Utopia signifies a firm conviction that present circumstances could be different; it harnesses man's powers of imagination of a better future. A revolutionary situation arises when possibilities for revolutionary change are at their maximum. The first symptoms begin to show when a given society gives evidence of a severe breakdown in its human and physical environment.

The symptoms are multiple. The most fundamental is the failure of the ruling élite or class to impose its set of values on the rest of the population. Such was the case in France before the Revolution. This particular revolution marked a turning-point in the history of social revolt because a substantial group of people gained a new historical consciousness. Refusing to accept the existing order of society as divinely willed or inevitable, they looked behind particular historical phenomena for their real human causes.

Thus the celebrated social question – the existence of vast discrimination in the distribution of wealth and income – called forth both a new explanation and a new tactic for its elimination. Because it was seen as the direct consequence of the accumulation of riches by a privileged minority, its elimination would come firstly through the overthrow of the entire system of values which justified privilege for a few.

The word 'ideology' was first coined by Antoine Destutt de Tracy in his book *Elements of Ideology* (1804). It was elaborated and made into an extremely effective tool of revolutionary struggle by Marx and Engels. Ideology, very simply, is the theoretical justification of vested interests. According to Marxism, these are always class interests. Karl Mannheim[1] believed that ideology is not simply a justification of power, which would not be difficult to defend on a theoretical basis, but much more subtly the idealization of a particular system or combination of values.

A typical example of how an ideology may work is that of the military *coup* in Chile in 1973 which overthrew the left-wing government of Salvador Allende. Both the *coup* and the subsequent regime have been sustained by an appeal to the traditional values of the Christian West.[2] However, having relentlessly eliminated all dissent and reinstated an economic system which entirely favours the Conservative owner class, the regime is in reality the antithesis of the 'open', democratic societies of the West, and its claim to uphold authentic Christian ideals is totally formal, traditional and superficial.

The development of the concept of ideology as an explanation for the persistency of autocracy and social inequality was made under the impulse of secular, liberal humanism, inspired by the Enlightenment notion of the natural equality of all human beings: 'we hold these truths to be self-evident, that all men are created equal.' (Constitution of the USA.)

The first result of the global questioning of values was the struggle for political independence. This began in North America, spread to the South American continent at the beginning of the last century, and since World War II has particular affected Africa and South East Asia.

These struggles have been called revolutionary because they have succeeded in forging new nations out of previously divided peoples. Liberation and unity have been the two main goals. Movements for independence began just as soon as an external or internal occupation of given territory could no longer be justified on ideological or pragmatic grounds. The self-evident injustice of foreign or minority rule has been a powerful factor in motivating liberation movements. Because of their sense of an indisputably righteous cause and the growing reaction of world opinion against every form of imperialism, they are ultimately more powerful than either a repressive police system (*e.g.* South Africa) or the intervention of a highly sophisti-

---

[1] K. Mannheim, *Ideology and Utopia: an Introduction to the Sociology of Knowledge* (Cambridge, 1955).　　[2] 'Los valores tradicionales del mundo occidental y cristiano.'

cated modern army (*e.g.* Vietnam).

Political independence from either external or internal foreign elements is a clear example of a new beginning. Independence Days are celebrated to prove it. However, whether this kind of independence implies real revolutionary change is another matter.

If the right to self-government and the freedom to develop institutions without outside interference is the mark of independence, then independence has been achieved today by most countries. Nevertheless, because more subtle forms of imperialism and dependence still exist, these same nations are still living in a pre-revolutionary situation.

One of the most potent forces for change today is the fact that many of the former colonial nations have become aware that they are now trapped by economic structures over which they have no real control. Independence and freedom are myths if internal political and social structures continue to depend upon external forces, which are no less real for not being strictly military.

In the last thirty years the critique of ideology has been systematically applied to the developed nations of the West (and East) in relation to their attitude towards the social problems of those countries where poverty exists on a massive scale. Since the Bandung Conference of non-aligned nations (1956), the emotive and yet real concept of the Third (and subsequently Fourth) World has emerged. Some people now suggest, though it is strongly denied by defenders of the present world economic order, that there is a greater ideological divide between the North and South than between the West and East.[3]

Consciousness of the way in which present economic imperialism works produces the necessary theoretical basis for revolutionary ferment. If other important elements are also present, this may develop into a revolutionary situation.

Unfortunately for the defenders of modern capitalism,[4] too many disagreeable facts about the history of its development and present

[3] One of the most significant political developments of the last few years may be the Chinese theory of super-power hegemonies: the 'Three-World Theory'. As self-appointed champion of the Third World against these hegemonies China is seeking a new re-alignment of political forces.

[4] An excellent exposition of the way the system works and its relation to political decision-making is given in Andrew Schonfield, *Modern Capitalism: the Changing Balance of Public and Private Power* (London, 1969[2]).

operation are now known. The West, which has enjoyed the consumer glut produced by capitalist expansion, has also experienced only one side of the system: its ability to create wealth. The Third World, by force of circumstances, has been brought face to face with the other side: its ability to create poverty.

Until recently little attention had been paid to the long-term historical cause of underdevelopment and stagnation in the economies of the Third World, but in the last twenty years or so two major theories have been advanced to account for it.

The first theory was popularized by W. Rostow.[5] He starts from the assumption that all countries were once equally poor and undeveloped. He is interested not so much in discovering why the Third World nations of today are caught in 'a low-level equilibrium trap' as how they may escape from it. The answer he proposes suggests a series of stages which will recapitulate the successful development of Western capitalism: *preconditioning*, including the application of technology to agriculture and industry; *take-off into sustained growth*, the gradual accumulation and reinvestment of capital in expanding industries; *drive to maturity*, the move from heavy industry to the production of goods and services for high-income consumers; *high mass-consumption*.

This theory may be correct as a description of the economic growth of the developed countries. As its sub-title suggests it is also a useful weapon in the ideological war to prevent non-aligned nations from adopting socialist systems. But as an explanation or cure for the real situation of the Third World it is inadequate, tendentious, or worse.[6]

---

[5] W. Rostow, *The Stages of Economic Growth: a Non-communist Manifesto* (Cambridge, 1961).

[6] One of the main difficulties of the theory is its lack of realism concerning the actual operation of international market forces. H. M. A. Onitiri in commenting on a paper by H. Myint, 'International Trade and the Developing Countries', says, 'Many of the restrictions imposed by the developed countries on the exports of the developing countries are designed precisely to obstruct desirable changes in the structures of international trade for reasons of politics, or in the interests of particular economic groups', P. A. Samuleson (ed.), *International Economic Relations* (London, 1972), p. 37. For a refutation of the orthodox equilibrium theory of comparative advantage in international trade, *cf*. J. Robinson and J. Eatwell, *An Introduction to Economics* (Maidenhead, 1973), pp. 330–336, and A. B. Atkinson, *The Economics of Inequality* (Oxford, 1975), chapter 12. The latter author shows why the distribution of wealth through aid programmes is ineffective and often increases the (social) problem it seeks to cure. He draws on the pioneering work of S. Kuznets in the field of economic growth and income inequality, *Modern Economic Growth* (New Haven, 1966).

The second theory[7] begins by exploring the real situation of the underdeveloped countries prior to the Western nations' take-off into sustained growth. The first discovery is that these countries, contrary to Rostow's view, were not always poor. In the 17th and early 18th century 'Asia was, for example, more advanced in both riches, commercial ability and mercantile knowledge (than Europe)'.[8] Moreover, because Asia possessed many goods that Europe needed, while Europe could offer Asia little trade in return, Europe could only secure her lines of supply by direct colonization: the British in India, the Dutch in Indonesia. In every case,[9] the standard of living of the colonized country declined sharply as their mineral resources were exploited for use in the growing industries of the West, as agricultural rights were removed or changed, and as their own industrial development was slowed down or halted.

The conclusions to be drawn from the survey are obvious, but too bitter to be easily accepted by those nations which have passed through Rostow's stages of development. Firstly, not all countries started from the same fixed point of underdevelopment; at the beginning of the 18th century, for example, India was economically more advanced than Europe.[10] Therefore, secondly, in the last 200 years many countries have become relatively poorer. There has been a kind of reverse growth in stages. Thirdly, the new poverty has been caused by direct exploitation enforced by military superiority.

Writing on the overall heritage of colonialism, the economist Daniel Fusfeld has this to say:

> These economic relationships of the colonial era, *which have persisted in varying degrees to the present*, were supplemented by political dominance on the part of the advanced countries. The citizens of colonial powers usually had special tax and legal privileges in the colonies and could acquire land and mineral rights on favoured terms. Banks and shipping companies had special privileges and often a monopolistic position. Tax systems and debt payments drained revenues to the colonial powers, whilst efforts were made to have the colonies pay the costs of their own administration. Tariff protection for industry in the colonies was usually

---

[7] We shall follow its exposition by K. B. Griffin, *Underdevelopment in Spanish America: an Interpretation* (London, 1969).

[8] *Ibid.*, p. 30.   [9] Griffin gives numerous examples, pp. 33–45.   [10] *Ibid*, p. 36.

denied, and the sort of economic development that would compete with home industry was hindered by colonial powers. Finally, little was done to promote the development of human resources, and the top administrative positions were reserved for citizens of the colonial powers.[11]

Investigation of the way in which present world economic structures have developed, like investigation of political structures in the past, unmasks the real causes of inequality and in the same way creates the necessary conditions for a revolutionary situation. The second symptom of a revolutionary situation, then, is the existence of an obviously righteous cause; in this case the knowledge that intolerable injustices have been perpetrated by some nations upon others.

The argument that we have outlined above concludes that Western economic growth has been achieved by a form of robbery. In the absence of some kind of reparation, alternative actions to gain a measure of economic independence become necessary: 'the answer is not more resources but the necessary structural transformation of a country in a conscious, explicit, ordered and rational way.'[12]

The third symptom arises when small but powerful groups strenuously oppose all attempts at putting this kind of alternative into practice. They operate either outside the law, in the form of paramilitary forces who dispense their own form of justice to those they regard as holding left-wing views, or under the cover of a kind of legality, usually through a *coup* by the armed forces (*e.g.* Brazil, 1964; Santo Domingo, 1966; Bolivia, 1971; Chile, 1973; Uruguay, 1974; Thailand, 1972 and 1976). Justification of the *coup* is nearly always the same: the breakdown of law and order; economic chaos; attempts at changing the constitution; and, above all, that mysterious entity, 'national security'.

In considering these four elements it is interesting to note that the military themselves often either arbitrarily change the constitution, or ignore it, and rarely, if ever, solve the pressing economic problems. Their accession to power is usually followed by a suspension of democratic institutions (*e.g.* political parties); the widespread removal of civil liberties (*e.g.* press freedom), and often by extreme,

---

[11] D. Fusfeld, *Economics* (Lexington, 1972), p. 901 (my italics).   [12] Griffin, p. 47.

repressive measures such as long periods of detention without com-munication and without trial, all of which also amounts to the effective breakdown of the rule of law.

All of these symptoms – the unmasking of legitimizing ideologies, the sense of a righteous cause and the repression unleashed by the backlash of threatened minorities – form part of a revolutionary situation. They do not, however, add up to a revolution. This depends upon two further factors.

The first is what Chalmers Johnson calls an 'accelerator'.[13] This is a particular event, or series of events, which enable an organized group of revolutionaries to take over the structures of power. In 1917 it was a power-vacuum caused in part by the defeat of the Russian army; in 1933 it was the sense of affront caused to German nationalism by defeat in war, by the evaporation in peace time of the savings of the middle classes and by an inept and indecisive government; in 1949 it was the successful culmination of a long guerrilla war in China, aided by the war with Japan; in 1959 it was the excessive corruption of the Batista regime in Cuba which united all opposition parties and made possible the successful conclusion of the Sierra Maestra guerrilla campaign.[14]

An accelerator cannot be created by the free decision of man. This is clear from the failure of every guerrilla movement in Latin America in the last decade to do anything more than superficially irritate the established powers, and from the way in which Western societies have absorbed various student and other middle-class protest move-ments without being forced to make any substantial change in their own structures. These latter movements have largely been spawned by conditions of affluence; they have been contained as a legitimate, if at times troublesome, expression of a pluralist society. An acceler-ator is present only when an unusual combination of different events happens at one particular time.

The second factor required for a genuine revolution is a concerted, concrete and feasible plan of action for the overthrow of one political order and its substitution by another. This raises serious doubts about the truly revolutionary nature of much self-justifying agita-

---

[13] C. Johnson, *Revolutionary Change* (London, 1968).

[14] An excellent analytical typology of 20th-century revolutions is given in the book by John Dunn, *Modern Revolutions* (Cambridge, 1972).

tion. The quotation by Hobsbawm at the beginning of the chapter refers to isolated acts of terrorism. He states further:

> That argument about 'individual terrorism' is an ancient one on the revolutionary left. It has divided Marxists from Anarchists and other terrorists since the latter part of the 19th century. It wasn't about violence as such, since revolutionary Marxists were quite prepared to use that. It was about what constituted revolutionary action.

Much of what passes for revolutionary action today, including guerrilla strikes, is little more than an isolated act of terrorism which is practically valueless from a strategic point of view. The question of a plan of action goes much deeper than a mere discussion of military and political tactics. It concerns the very meaning of revolutionary change and the necessary conditions for its implementation. Jacques Ellul concludes that no recent manifestation of revolutionary action can really be called revolutionary,[15] for either the objective conditions for change in a given society were not present (as, for example, in the Western nations today or Czechoslovakia in 1968), or the so-called revolutions, even when advocating 'permanent revolution' (as in the case of the Chinese Cultural Revolution) have failed to fulfil their promises. For these reasons Ellul believes that all revolutions up to now should be understood as revolts in which man's perennial struggle against evil becomes manifest in a particularly dramatic and usually violent form.

So when we speak of a revolutionary situation we do not imply that revolutions which spring from them necessarily change things for the better. We have simply tried to point out some of the symptoms which generally precede revolutionary actions, even if these are neither successful nor justified. Later on we shall try to evaluate the motives and substance of modern revolution.

---

[15] J. Ellul, *De la révolution aux révoltes* (Paris, 1972). However, one serious weakness in Ellul's study is his failure to define adequately what *he* means by revolution. We simply know what he does not mean. His account of the failure of revolutionary movements, though basically sound, might be accused of 'perfectionism'. He gives the impression of withholding support from any movement for fundamental change unless its purposes and achievements pass a very rigorous examination. Though we should carefully weigh the odds of producing something less evil on the other side of revolution, Ellul's stance could block all initiative to break out of a particular, vicious circle of injustice and repression.

Chapter Three

Revolutionary theology appears on stage

All men are sinners before a righteous God, but not all men are victims in an unjust society.
William Lazareth, Foreword to J. Miguez,
Doing Theology in a Revolutionary Situation (1975).

Revolutionary theology has been born in the post-war period as the result of a bad conscience and with a transforming mission in mind. An increasing number of Christian thinkers from various parts of the world church have, in the last two decades, begun to challenge modern theology's apparent indifference to social questions. Taking up the problems posed by a grossly unjust distribution of wealth between nations and individuals in the shrinking world of today, and by seemingly immovable, privileged structures of power, they have become the contemporary church's conscience in the field of social ethics.

This challenge has evolved into a fundamental questioning of the direction in which theology has been moving in recent years. Revolutionary theology has not simply been content to fill a gap left by academic theology; in some of its forms, particularly Black Theology and Liberation Theology, it has cast doubt upon the whole purpose and method of theology as it stands today. Certain modern theological emphases have been interpreted as supplying ideological props for an attitude of indifference towards social and political change. It is this sense of mission towards theology itself which makes revolutionary theology particularly interesting and important for the church today.

Following the appearance of Jürgen Moltmann's epoch-making book *Theology of Hope* (1965), revolution has become probably the most live issue in contemporary theology. However, theological interest in revolution antedates Moltmann's study by at least ten years. Though it is difficult to date its origin precisely, revolutionary theology was born when Christian thinkers discovered the political and economic reality of the Third World. This first happened when Richard Shaull, a missionary in Latin America, produced his personal theological response to a continent in crisis.[1]

Shaull gradually became aware of three interrelated facts: firstly, that revolution in Latin America was both a necessity and a possibility; secondly, that traditional Christian social thought was unable to interpret the phenomenon adequately and, thirdly, that the Christian message nevertheless 'has tremendous political consequences, it offers us the possibilities for understanding and solving the principal problems of revolution not easily found elsewhere.'[2]

Shaull, and those who followed him, gave Christian social thought a new impetus and a new direction. He was clearly indebted to those who, during the first half of the present century, were outstanding in their attempts to relate the gospel to contemporary political reality: for example, Walter Rauschenbusch; Reinhold Niebuhr; Karl Barth and Dietrich Bonhoeffer, to mention the giants.[3]

Rauschenbusch and the social gospel (1861–1918)

Rauschenbusch is associated with a movement of social reform in North America which spanned the second half of the 19th century and the first third of the 20th.[4] The movement's basic premise was that man's collective organizations, and not just himself personally, stand under judgment. This belief gives the church a basis from which to move beyond an individual ethic to a social critique of certain institutions such as, for example, capitalism, the state and the labour movement. Moreover, because social good and evil are col-

---

[1] R. Shaull, *Encounter with Revolution* (New York, 1955).   [2] *Ibid.*, p. 115.
[3] In a fuller treatment than we can undertake here the names of N. Berdyaev and William Temple ought to be added. We are not aware, however, that either of them particularly influenced the development of revolutionary theology. Their main contributions to social thinking are contained in N. Berdyaev, *The Realm of Spirit and the Realm of Caesar* (New York, 1952); W. Temple, *The Hope of a New World* (London, 1940) and *Christianity and the Social Order* (Harmondsworth, 1942).
[4] Here I follow the account given in P. A. Carter, *The Decline and Revival of the Social Gospel: Social and Political Liberalism in American Protestant Churches 1920–40* (Ithaca, 1956); *cf.* also J. Neal Hughley, *Trends in Protestant Social Idealism* (New York, 1948).

lective, and because the Christian inevitably shares in a collective whole, he is called to work for the reconstruction of society as part of his Christian obedience.

In *A Theology for the Social Gospel* (1917), Rauschenbusch[5] describes how the concepts of spiritual regeneration and the Kingdom of God could be socialized and institutionalized. Those who were involved in the movement differed over the amount of change that might be needed for the social order to be genuinely regenerated. Some were content with substantial reforms (*e.g.* the paying of just wages); a smaller group under the influence of Marxism pressed for a more radical type of society (*e.g.* the abolition of the wage-system). Both groups agreed that capitalism as it stood was a formidable obstacle to the implementing of the Kingdom[6].

Believing that Jesus' ethical imperatives should be applied to society as it exists, American Churches *found* the social gospel in the course of working out the logic of an evangelistic quest for a 'Christian America'.[7]

Convinced that something ought and could be done to remedy the ills of society, the 'social gospellers' were involved shortly after World War 1 in bringing about substantial changes in the conditions of American labour, in the move to extend legislation on civil liberties and in international relations. However, they tended to neglect the complicated problems of relating means to ends and were much too optimistic in thinking that Americans, *en masse*, would adopt and practise Christian ideals. Here they neglected to take into consideration the significant history of violence and oppression in their own American past, and the apparent ease with which vast sectors of the Christian public were able to use their beliefs to suppress practices which might challenge their right to the 'good life' they enjoyed. The failure on the part of many American Christians to translate ideals into practice was seen, many years later, in the test case of civil liberties for minority groups. It was never really intended, apparently, that the 'American dream' should become a universal reality.

[5] He also wrote *Christianity and the Social Crisis* (1907) and *Christianising the Social Order* (1909).

[6] Carter, *op. cit.*, p. 13.

[7] *Ibid.*, p. 10.

Reinhold Niebuhr (1892–1964)

Niebuhr in his advocacy of Christian political realism pressed these particular weaknesses of the social gospel movement. He began, however, to define his own theological thinking on political matters in a different set of historical circumstances, those of the 'great depression'.[8]

Initially, he was influenced by Marxism. Society is immoral, he states, because it is geared to the preservation of power for only one sector – the bourgeoisie who rule it. The only human beings really capable of 'morality' are those who have no vested interests in present society to corrupt them, *i.e.* the proletariat. Only they can bring about an approximate social justice. Hence, only by adopting a socialist form of society can the gap between moral man and immoral society be bridged. In 1931 Niebuhr helped to establish the Fellowship of Socialist Christians.

However, even in his socialist days, Niebuhr never attempted to identify the Kingdom with the achievement of radical social change. He argued that, because the ruling élite will not surrender their privileges voluntarily, such change can happen only through violence. But, violence can do no more than re-order society for the benefit of the majority; it cannot establish the Kingdom.

As the momentous forces of tyranny began to spread their tentacles over Europe and Russia, Niebuhr shifted his theological emphasis to include a critique of all utopianisms.

Firstly, he criticized those who believed that Marxism still offered real possibilities for a better social order. Marxism, he asserted, like liberalism, presupposes 'moral' man and, thus, after the revolution a 'moral society'. But such a society had never existed and could not ever be expected to do so from the perspective of Christian revelation. Just as Marxism denied the historical reality of original sin, so original sin contradicted the Marxist account of history. In the light of the acts of immoral man, Marxism was a wildly optimistic, social utopianism.

Niebuhr's polemic was also directed against the growing tendency of some American churches to repudiate, on pacifist grounds,

---

[8] *Cf.* R. Niebuhr, *Moral Man and Immoral Society* (New York, 1932).

America's possible involvement in war with Germany. In his book, *Christianity and Power Politics*,[9] he accuses the modern espousers of pacifism of teaching a perfectionism which glosses over the fact that sin introduces real, deep elements of conflict into the world. They fail, he says, to make a proper distinction 'between the ethic of the Kingdom which makes no concession to human sin, and political strategies which, assuming human sinfulness, seek to secure the relatively highest measure of peace and justice among selfish and sinful men.'[10] These strategies necessarily involve balancing power with power. This balance of power may be inferior to the harmony of love, but without it love may become a screen which hides injustice.

Niebuhr's adoption of a pessimistic view of human nature made him theologically wary of the idealism of Christian pacifism and the utopianism of both the political left and the extreme right. He inclined, as a result, to a defence of the gains of the democratic way of life against all tyrannies (Communism or National Socialism) and all anarchies (war and rebellion):[11] 'I hope that democratic nations will not lightly sacrifice the virtues of democracy for the sake of escaping its defects.'[12]

Nevertheless, Niebuhr's prophetic consciousness never allowed him to abandon a penetrating critique of these defects. He sums up his convictions on the subject in this way:

> Upon the historical level, where all things are relative . . . distinctions between the relatively good and the relatively evil are very important.[13]

Like the exponents of the social gospel before him, Niebuhr reflected the condition of the world in which he lived in his theological assessment of social action. If the social gospel clearly demonstrated its debt to the final surge of 19th-century liberal, optimistic belief in human evolutionary progress, Niebuhr incorporated into his critique of society the folly and incompetence of liberal economic policies which led to the massive unemployment and consequent

[9] New York, 1940.   [10] *Ibid.*, p. 11.

[11] Further, *cf.* R. Niebuhr, *The Children of Light and the Children of Darkness* (New York, 1944); *Christian Realism and Political Problems* (New York, 1954).

[12] R. Niebuhr, *Christianity and Power Politics*, p. 28.

[13] R. Niebuhr, *Reflections on the End of an Era* (New York, 1934), p. 170.

suffering of the early 1930s.

A pessimistic view of human nature does not, therefore, as has often been suggested, lead one automatically to accept that market-capitalism is best able to adjust to, and deal with, mankind's basic and wilful selfishness. Berdyaev, for example, has argued that the all-pervading presence of sin in society means that we should attempt to change it in a socialist direction. Contrary to the oft-stated belief, it is socialism, rather than capitalism, that is born of a pessimistic view of human nature:

> It is the *bourgeois* ideology of Capitalism which has been optimistic and believed in a natural harmony arising out of the conflict of private interests.[14]

Of course, Berdyaev made it clear that for him Communism was not the same as socialism, for the simple reason that whatever has to be carried out by massive coercion, according to the fiat of an élite minority, cannot be a human utopia.

Faced with the great depression, Niebuhr would have been inclined to agree with the need to curb the power of capitalist industry to determine the shape of the nation's economic life. But, faced with the rise of Nazi Germany and Fascist Italy, he would also have been aware of the danger of centralizing power too completely in the hands of the state. These two great realities of the 1930s pose quite starkly the different ways in which power can come to be exerted without accountability. In Niebuhr's thinking the greater the immorality of society the greater the responsibility of Christians to be involved in it in a non-ideological fashion, rejecting easy utopian solutions on the one hand, and on the other struggling to change what needs to be changed within a democratic framework.

Karl Barth (1886–1968)

One of the great influences on Niebuhr's thought was the dialectical theology of Karl Barth. Nevertheless, their theological thinking on the most important political issues of their time by no means coincided.

[14] N. Berdyaev, *The Russian Revolution* (Ann Arbor, 1966), p. 54 (originally published in 1931).

Karl Barth's 'social philosophy' is a complex amalgam of apparently contradictory ideas, whose theological relevance has been hotly contested. The ideas are distributed mainly in theological essays[15] and letters.[16] His theological encounter with National Socialism and his post-war reflections on Communism[17] form the substance of his thought in this area.

Barth passed through three stages in his assessment of the 20th century's two most powerful ideologies. His initial reaction to Hitler's *Volkstum* philosophy was not total opposition. Rather, he was disturbed by the subtle way in which the Nazis sought to harness the state church to their cause. He feared that Christians would be tempted to recognize an external authority and an objective revelation which did not come directly from Jesus Christ as 'the one Word of God'; and would thereby lose 'their theological existence.' After the war, Barth explained why he reacted so vigorously and decisively to the Nazi menace:

> The Central and Western European peoples – first Germany, then the others – had succumbed to Hitler's spell. He had become a spiritual, and almost everywhere, a political source of temptation. . . . It was at that time that I made my various attempts to make the Church ready for action against the temptations of National Socialism.[18]

Later Barth's opposition deepened and became more complete. He was personally involved in the events which led up to the establishment of a new 'Caesaropapacy':

> Toward the end of 1934, as a professor at Bonn, Barth was required to take the oath of allegiance to Adolf Hitler. He was ready to do so if only

---

[15] K. Barth, *Evangelium und Gesetz* (Munich, 1935); *Trouble and Promise in the Struggle of the Church in Germany* (Oxford, 1938); *Rechtfertigung und Recht* (Zürich, 1938); *Against the Stream: Shorter Post-War Writings* (including his celebrated 'The Christian Community and the Civil Community') (New York, 1954).

[16] K. Barth, *The Christian Cause* (New York, 1941); 'A Letter to American Christians', *Christendom*, VIII, 1943, pp. 441–458.

[17] Two accounts of Barth's social thought are particularly succinct and helpful: C. C. West, *Communism and the Theologians: Study of an Encounter* (London, 1958), pp. 177–325; Will Herberg, 'The Social Philosophy of Karl Barth' in *Community, State and Church* (New York, 1960).

[18] K. Barth, *Against the Stream*, pp. 114–115.

it was understood that his allegiance to Hitler was limited by his higher loyalty to God; but this the government refused.[19]

Barth's theological indictment of Nazi totalitarianism is set out in his essay *Rechtfertigung und Recht* (1938), written from the comparative safety of Basle. He sees an absolute rejection of Hitler's claims as part of 'the service which the Church owes the State', a service to be inferred from a careful study of Romans 13:1–7. He believes the state, normally, has the right to make claims on its citizens, including oath-taking and military service.[20]

It is quite another matter whether the State has any right to try to strengthen its authority by making any kind of *inward* claim upon its subjects and its citizens; that is whether it has any right to demand from them a particular philosophy of life (*Weltanschauung*), or at least sentiments and reactions dominated by a particular view imposed by the State from without. According to the New Testament, the only answer to this question is an unhesitating 'No!' . . . Here we are very near the menace of 'the Beast out of the Abyss' . . . From Romans 13 it is quite clear that love is not one of the duties we owe the State. When the State begins to claim 'love', it is in the process of becoming a Church, the Church of a false God, and thus an unjust State.[21]

In his confrontation with Communism Barth has been chided (by Brunner, Niebuhr and West among others) for not applying the same theological insights which he developed in the struggle against Nazi totalitarianism.[22] His reply was that Communism does not pose the same kind of temptation or threat to Western Churches.[23] Clearly, he was no defender of Communism; neither did he see it as such an unmitigated evil as Nazism.[24]

[19] Herberg, *op. cit.*, p. 41.
[20] There is a very thorough discussion of Barth's rather unusual attitude towards war in J. H. Yoder, *Karl Barth and the Problem of War* (New York, 1970).
[21] Herberg, *op. cit.*, pp. 76–77.
[22] *Cf.* Emil Brunner, 'An Open Letter to Karl Barth' in *Against the Stream*; Reinhold Niebuhr, 'Why is Barth Silent on Hungary?', *The Christian Century*, 23 January 1957; West, *Communism and the Theologians*, p. 304.
[23] *Cf.* 'The Christian Community in the Midst of Political Change' in *Against the Stream*.
[24] *Ibid.*, p. 140.

West thinks the contradiction in Barth's attitude is due, firstly, to his poor information and 'ineptitude . . . in the field of social and political decisions'[25] and, secondly, to his attempt to incorporate his theology of the state into a Christocentric theology of redemption. Comparing the theological differences between Barth and Niebuhr he has this brief but penetrating comment to make:

> He (Niebuhr) is, in short . . . more acutely aware than Barth of the ways of God with human structures of power, order and justice, precisely because, or so it seems, of his refusal to place the whole political process from the beginning under the order of redemption. Barth seems, because of his all-embracing grace, to neglect his responsibility for that difficult empirical analysis of real human relations, most especially in politics, which the Christian, just because of his faith, should take more seriously than all others.[26]

Barth's theological understanding of the state, though making him sympathetic to some form of socialism, also caused him to oppose any revolutionary movement aiming at total change. His idea of the 'righteous State' (and here he coincides with Niebuhr) is of a state organized on democratic lines:

> I should say we are justified, from the point of view of exegesis, in regarding the 'democratic conception of the State' as a justifiable expansion of the thought of the New Testament. . . . Christians must not only endure the earthly State . . . they must *will* it, . . . they cannot will it as a 'Pilate' State, but as a just State.[27]

Dietrich Bonhoeffer (1906–1945)

Bonhoeffer grew up, theologically, in the shadow of Barth. Until the very end of his short, productive and embattled life he acknow-

[25] West, *op. cit.*, p. 304.

[26] *Ibid.*, p. 314. Perhaps the most significant aspect of Barth's different approach to the two totalitarianisms is that he was vitally involved with the first and almost completely abstracted from the second. A theologian's personal situation profoundly affects his theological stance, as we shall see.

[27] Herberg, *op. cit.*, pp. 147–148.

ledged Barth's lasting influence upon his theological pilgrimage. At the same time, Bonhoeffer was always an independent and original thinker. This is shown especially by his later writings,[28] which reflect the very particular circumstances of his life.

Any attempt to systematize his theological reflections on the radical political upheavals through which he lived, and whose victim he eventually became, is probably invalid. Instead we shall adopt the style of his own occasional thoughts from prison and offer certain impressions on his theological grapplings with political reality.[29]

John Phillips believes Bonhoeffer moved through two distinct phases. In the first, following his first visit to the USA in 1930, he was absorbed by the theological controversy within the German Church which followed the Barmen Declaration of 31 May 1934. In the second, following his second visit to the USA in 1939, his thought was conditioned by his involvement in the resistance movement to Hitler and his subsequent imprisonment in Berlin on 5 April 1943.

In the first stage, then, Bonhoeffer came to regard the Nazi regime as an embodiment of Antichrist. This forced him to rethink radically the classical Lutheran doctrine of the two kingdoms, and particularly to consider the boundaries of the church in its relationship to the unique and total Lordship of Christ.

He instinctively (or prophetically) mistrusted Hitler from the beginning. In a radio broadcast[30] two days after Hitler became Chancellor of Germany (1 February 1933), Bonhoeffer distinguished two groups of Christians in Germany, those who held to only one *ultimate* authority (God) and those who turned the *penultimate* (a human leader) into the ultimate:

If he (the leader) allows himself to surrender to the wishes of his follow-ers, who would always make him their idol – then the image of the

[28] The Manuscripts written from 1939–42 and later published as *Ethik* (1949) (English trans. *Ethics*, London, 1955) and the *Letters and Papers from Prison* (London, 1959).

[29] We have consulted particularly John A. Phillips, *Christ for Us in the Theology of Dietrich Bonhoeffer* (New York, 1967); *No Rusty Swords*, Vol I; *The Way to Freedom*, Vol II; and *True Patriotism*, Vol. III, from *The Collected Works of Dietrich Bonhoeffer* (1965, 1966, 1968); *Letters and Papers from Prison*.

[30] *No Rusty Swords, op. cit.*, pp. 190–204.

Leader (*Führer*) will pass over into the image of the misleader (*Verführer*, seductor). . . . Leaders or offices which set themselves up as gods mock God and the individual who stands alone before him, *and must perish* (my italics).

The German Christians, who by 1933 dominated the state Lutheran Church, had been seduced and, consequently, were mocking God. Following the Barmen Declaration, Bonhoeffer states categorically that the *Reich* Church

> can no longer claim to compose the Church of Christ nor any part of it;[31] the Confessing Church confesses *in concretissimo* against the German Christian Church and against the neo-pagan divinization of the creature.[32]

In this first stage Bonhoeffer states, probably as clearly as any Christian has ever done, the theological reasons for resisting every tyrannical messianism. His famous treatise against all false political and ideological compromises, *The Cost of Discipleship*, reflects the implications of this resistance.

The second stage seems to belong to a different man. In many ways this was true, for his outward circumstances had changed considerably. He had become identified with a circle of people who, eventually, decided to assassinate Hitler; he was physically removed from all pastoral and teaching contact with the church and, in prison, he was unable to express himself freely on the great political issues of the moment. Suddenly, as a bolt out of the blue, he announced his first tentative steps towards 'religionless' Christianity.[33]

Conscious, perhaps, of the inevitable overthrow of National Socialism, he began again to view the world, and therefore the political sphere, in a more positive light. His distinction between the ultimate and the penultimate seemed less severe. His North German attachment to the earth, though not in the idolatrous Fascist sense, and his delight in cultural pursuits made him, basically, a

---

[31] *Cf.* Phillips, p. 22.   [32] *No Rusty Swords*, pp. 337–338.
[33] The first reference seems to be in the letter of 30 April 1944: 'You would be surprised and perhaps disturbed if you knew how my ideas on theology are taking shape. . . . What is the significance of a Church in a religionless world?. . . How do we speak in secular fashion of God?'

world-affirming person. These traits, in spite of his situation, shine again in the writings from prison.

It is not surprising that he had an unusually high regard for the Old Testament, due in part, no doubt, to his inflexible defence of the Jewish people. From the Old Testament he learnt of the importance of *historical* redemption and the unfragmented nature of life. The former is 'redemption on this side of death, whereas the myths of salvation are concerned to offer men deliverance from death';[34] the latter 'denies our distinction of outer and inner. . . . It is always concerned with *anthropos teleios*, the *whole* man. . . . It is quite unbiblical to suppose that a "good intention" is enough'.[35]

For Bonhoeffer, Christian faith could be meaningful only in the midst of life, at the very centre of man's social concerns. Thus, a large part of what he meant by 'religionless' Christianity is, I believe, a rejection of every kind of spirit/matter dualism:

> In what way are we in a religionless and secular sense Christians, not conceiving of ourselves religiously as specially favoured, but as wholly belonging to the world? Then Christ is no longer an object of religion, but something quite different, indeed and in truth the Lord of the World.[36]

Finally, Bonhoeffer was aware that some kind of new social order should be built from the shattered ruins of European civilization. Though certain facets of his life and thought might be considered inimical to a serious concern about social questions – for example, by upbringing and temperament he was a patrician, and he never reflected much on the social challenge of Marxism[37] – nevertheless, suffering had taught him to accept a different future ordering of society:

> It should not be difficult for us to forfeit our privileges, recognizing the justice of history. We may have to face events and changes which run counter to our rights and wishes. But, if so, we shall not give way to bitterness and foolish pride, but consciously submit to divine judgment,

---

[34] Letter of 27 June 1944.   [35] Letter of 8 July 1944.   [36] Letter of 30 April 1944.
[37] *Cf.* Peter Berger, 'Sociology and Ecclesiology' in Martin Marty (ed.), *The Place of Bonhoeffer* (New York, 1962), pp. 58ff.

and thus prove our worthiness to survive by identifying ourselves generously and unselfishly with the life of the community and the interests of our fellowmen.[38]

At the end of the 1950s two independent groups began to reflect, in different circumstances and with different aims in view, on the challenge of secular, revolutionary thought and action.

In Paris in 1959 a group of French Communists and French Jesuits began informal and unofficial discussions on the relationship between Marxist theory and Roman Catholic doctrine. Further contacts between Roman Catholics and Communists were indirectly encouraged by Pope John XXIII's two social encyclicals, *Mater et Magister* (1961) and *Pacem in Terris* (1963). The latter, for example, against previous Church tradition, recognizes that Marxists, despite their ideology, could be inspired by worthy motives. The official stamp of approval for dialogue was given in Vatican II by the document *Gaudium et Spes*. It cautiously admits the possibility of legitimate revolution (para. 74), recognizes that the present world economic system causes inherent injustices (paras. 63, 65, 67) and that property has a social end (para. 69). More significantly, perhaps, it acknowledges that Christians may be partly responsible for the birth of atheism, which is 'a violent protest against . . . the absolute character with which certain human values are unduly invested' (para. 19). Therefore, finally, it encourages dialogue with men who profess atheism, even while rejecting it 'root and branch' (para. 21).[39]

On the other side, Marxists who had denounced Stalinism showed a greater willingness to discuss common issues with opponents. Among them was the Czech, Machovec, who in the early 1960s organized seminars on Christianity and Marxism at which men like Hromadka, Gollwitzer, Rahner, Moltmann and Metz on the Christian side, and Bloch, Fromm, Garaudy,[40] Radice and Gardavsky[41] on the other, took part. These seminars culminated in a large Christian-Marxist encounter at Marienbad in the spring of 1967, the first

[38] 'Thoughts on the Baptism of D. W. R.' in *Letters and Papers from Prison*, p. 159.

[39] For the text *cf.* W. M. Abbott (ed.) *The Documents of Vatican II* (New York, 1966).

[40] Author of the books *From Anathema to Dialogue* (New York, 1966); *The Turning Point of Socialism* (London, 1970) and *Marxism in the Twentieth Century* (London, 1970).

[41] Author of the book *God is Not Yet Dead* (Harmondsworth, 1973).

ever to be held on Communist territory.[42] Similar dialogues were organized in France and Italy.[43]

During the same period in Latin America groups of Protestants and Roman Catholics began to reflect theologically on their personal experience of the so-called 'revolution of rising expectations'.

Among the former, Shaull was the initiator and the Church and Society in Latin America group[44] the institutional catalyst of a new agenda for theological thought.[45] According to Santa Ana, the first editor of the journal *Iglesia y Sociedad (Church and Society)*, renewed reflection from within a commitment to change in Latin America should centre on three fundamental problems: the practical and theological relationship between the church and the world; the interaction between faith and ideology; and the concrete demands of Christian discipleship. The subsequent thought of the ISAL group strongly affected the findings of the 1966 WCC-sponsored conference on church and society held in Geneva. The tone was set for a new understanding of the relationship between a theological account of freedom and secular manifestations of revolution.

Among the Roman Catholic group were the forerunners, up to 1966, of the theology of liberation.[46] Like their European colleagues, they were encouraged by the Pope's social encyclicals to adopt a greater openness to secular thinking. They were also stimulated by contact with left-wing intellectuals to revise, from top to bottom, their church's entire teaching and involvement in social issues.

At a later date, under the same impact of the discovery of the Third World as a particular social problem, evangelical Christians

[42] *Cf.* Peter Hebblethwaite, 'Introduction' in Machovec, *A Marxist looks at Jesus* (London, 1976).

[43] *Cf. El hombre cristiano y el hombre marxista* (Barcelona, 1967); and *El dialogo de la época* (Buenos Aires, 1965). For the content of the dialogue and the presuppositions which made it possible *cf.* my article, 'The Meaning of Man in the Debate between Christianity and Marxism', *Themelios*, 1, 1976, pp. 41–43, and H. Cox, 'New Phase in the Marxist-Christian Encounter', *Christianity and Crisis*, XXV, 18, pp. 226–230.

[44] Iglesia y Sociedad en América Latina (ISAL).

[45] *Cf.* J. de Santa Ana, 'The Influence of Bonhoeffer on the Theology of Liberation', *ER*, 27, April 1975; J. Miguez, 'Visión del cambio social y sus tareas desde las Iglesias no católicas' in *Fe cristiana y cambio social en América Latina* (Salamanca, 1973); J. A. Kirk, 'La interpretación de la Biblia en el Protestantismo latinoamericano', in P. Savage (ed.), *Debate contemporaneo sobre la Biblia* (Barcelona, 1973).

[46] *Cf.* chapter 8 of this book, and J. A. Kirk, *Liberation Theology: an Evangelical View from the Third World* (London, 1979) for the historical antecedents of this movement.

have adopted a less individualistic approach to the implications of faith in Christ and a greater awareness of the corporate nature of human evil than was formerly the case.[47]

---

[47] The following documents represent a progressive opening by evangelicals to the fact that the gospel also speaks about justice and liberation for the poor: *Keele '67: The National Evangelical Anglican Statement* (London, 1967), pp. 26–30; *The Chicago Declaration of Christians for Social Action* (1973); 'The Theological Implications of Radical Discipleship: A Response to Lausanne' in *Let the Earth Hear his Voice* (Minneapolis, 1975), pp. 1294–1296; *The Nottingham Statement* (London, 1977); *Gospel and Culture: The Willowbank Report* (Wheaton, 1978), pp. 25–26; (London 1978), pp. 36–37. It is of course true to say that individual evangelicals have gone further in statements and writings than is often possible in representative gatherings: for example, R. Padilla (ed.), *The New Face of Evangelicalism* (London, 1976).

PART II

*Revolutionary theologies in
the three worlds*

Chapter Four

Western Europe:
pragmatic atheism and theoretical Marxism

It is important to be able to decide what constitutes the fullness of historical living. Here Marxism postulates itself as a substitute for Christianity. The Church only has the Gospel, which is not a message which could have been invented. The Gospel speaks of the 'new man', but in its own terms.

Helmut Gollwitzer,
The Marxist Criticism of Religion and the Christian Faith (1967).

We shall now try to synthesize the fertile views of three important thinkers, but before doing so we need to say why we have selected them.

The choice of *Moltmann* really needs no defence. He is by now the best-known, one of the most prolific, and certainly one of the most creative of a generation of German theologians who have begun to reflect seriously upon the social nature of Christian faith in the modern world.

Metz is in a sense his Roman Catholic counterpart. Like Moltmann he has engaged in dialogue with Marxists. He has written extensively on the political implications of the Christian world-view, as he understands it, and on the ideological nature of the church. Together with Rahner he has been singled out by the theologians of liberation as the best representative of a particular tradition of political theology within European Roman Catholicism.

Gollwitzer is probably the least known of the three. He has come to discuss the issues surrounding revolution through the traumatic experiences of the German Confessing Church and a prisoner-of-war camp in Russia. His book, *The Marxist Criticism of Religion and the Christian Faith*, has become a minor classic. Some think he is the most original of the European theologians writing on revolution.

Jürgen Moltmann

Theology of Hope[1] marks a watershed in European theology, the beginning of a new theological consciousness. The break with the existentialist school of Bultmann and the post-Bultmannians goes deep.[2] Philosophically it signifies a rejection of the Kantian distinction between subjectivity and objectivation in the approach to history. In seeking for a meaning in history beyond that provided by the individual who studies it, Moltmann follows the Hegelian historiographical tradition. Theologically, it signifies a decisive rupture with the recurring influence of the Greek philosophical tradition on contemporary theology.

Strongly emphasizing the future as the principal factor which determines the process of time, and stressing the language of promise, hope and the new creation, Moltmann displays his conviction that Christian theology must begin from the Hebrew view of history. The fundamental difference between Israelite faith and the 'epiphanic' religions in general, and Greek philosophy in particular, 'does not lie in the assertion of the divine "revelation" as such, but in the different ways of conceiving . . . the self-manifestation of the deity.' For the epiphanic religions 'any place in the world can become . . . the pictorial transparency of the deity,' but for biblical faith 'promise is determinative of what is said of the revealing God.' This distinction implies that 'every theological view of biblical revelation contains implicitly a governing view of eschatology.'[3]

Again, the difference between Moltmann and the existentialists is not over the use of the word eschatology, but over its relationship to human history. For the existentialists, only the present moment of history is significant. Hence, eschatology is wholly realized as the impact of transcendence upon this moment of history. But, for Moltmann, because the whole of history is pregnant with meaning,

---

[1] J. Moltmann, *Theologie der Hoffnung* (Munich, 1965).
[2] *Cf.* W. Nicholls, *The Pelican Guide to Modern Theology, Vol. I: Systematic and Philosophical Theology* (Harmondsworth, 1969), pp. 338–340.
[3] All quotes from *Theology of Hope*, p. 43.

eschatology is the still-future reality of human history directed according to God's promises. Humanity now stands historically on this side of the resurrection, so that history is meaningful only in the light of the coming Kingdom which this event has already inaugurated. Because their faith points towards the promised future, Christians can never find final significance in any one moment or movement of history.

Moltmann criticizes existentialist theology for running away from history by trying to assert the transcendence of present existence against the seeming deceit of Christian hope.[4] Because of this indifference to the future of world history (*i.e.* to the liberation of the enslaved creation), existentialist theology is politically conservative: 'Bultmann replaces the theodicy question – the search for a just world – with the question of a quest for the identity of one's own existence'; in the place of 'the quest for the sense and purpose of world history' he has substituted 'a search for the meaning of the history of existence.'[5]

Challenged by Ernst Bloch's monumental secular theology of hope, *Das Prinzip Hoffnung*,[6] Moltmann began to think about the theological significance of post-industrial society whose future seems so highly problematical.

He describes Western technological society as officially optimistic, convinced of its ability to resolve recurrent crises and devoted to the god of 'success'. This position is upheld at the very high cost of consigning past horrors (particularly Auschwitz and Hiroshima) to oblivion, and being apathetic about the miseries created by its present conservative use of power.

Political and social conservatism is caused by fear of a genuinely open future (*i.e.* one open to innovation and the unexpected). This human *Angst*, Moltmann believes, is not simply an ontological problem which man tries to solve by adhering to the present order as a defence against the future; it is something which finds a real, concrete

---

[4] *Ibid*, pp. 29–30.

[5] 'Towards a Political Hermeneutic of the Gospel', *USQR*, 23, 1968, pp. 308–311.

[6] Berlin, 1959. The work has never been translated. However, shorter works by Bloch have been collected in *Man on His Own: Essays in the Philosophy of Religion* (New York, 1970); *On Karl Marx* (London, 1971); *Atheism in Christianity* (New York, 1972). *Cf.* also Moltmann's contribution to the E. Bloch Festschrift, *E. Bloch zu ehren* (Frankfurt, 1965): 'Die Kategorie *Novum* in der christlichen Theologie.'

expression in the fetishism of the consumer ideal.[7] Fear of the future leads man to adopt an unhistorical attitude towards the world, which is neither 'a heaven of self-realization nor a hell of self-alienation', but 'a battlefield in the struggle between inhumanity and humanity.'[8]

The church's neglect of the future as the sphere of God's renewing action has meant that modern eschatologies, of which Marxism is still the most influential, have become secular. Because Christians believed in a 'God without future', those who were concerned for the earth's future looked for a 'future without God.[9]

Moltmann shares with Marxism the following convictions:

(a) that to overcome present contradictions and sufferings is both necessary and possible;

(b) that hope is a call to see beyond existing perspectives for change, and a basis for constructing a new image of society which will challenge the claim that present society has reached a harmonious state;

(c) that a purely factual, technical analysis of present reality is an inadequate basis for change;

(d) that religion is the mythological protest against real affliction;

(e) that modern man's alienation and oppression are due to the economic forces which dominate him.

Nevertheless, he strongly criticizes Marxists for substituting for God's open future the closed future of a mythological 'golden age'. God's future is not renovation (*futurum*), but transformation (*adventus*).[10] In his (theological) criticism of Marxism, Moltmann displays the revolutionary scope of his theology.

His approach to the West European tradition of Marxism is not intended 'to assist in a reflection on Marxism, but to forward its release to be itself, and to achieve the humanity which is contained in its humanistic traditions, but is also concealed by these.'[11] He therefore makes the following main criticisms of Marxism:

(a) It is irretrievably tied to an inadequate humanistic basis inherited from the Enlightenment through Feuerbach. From these two sources have arisen the twin utopian ideals of the 'authentic' society

---

[7] Cf. *Theology of Hope*, pp. 19–22; 91–94; 'Liberation in the Light of Hope' in *ER*, 26, July 1974, p. 413; 'Religion, Revolution and Future' in *The Future of Hope* (Philadelphia, 1970).

[8] J. Moltmann, *Man: Christian Anthropology in the Conflicts of the Present* (London, 1974), p. 36.   [9] 'Religion, Revolution and Future'.   [10] *Ibid.*   [11] *Man*, p. 59.

and the 'divinization' of man.

(b) Its analysis of human alienation is too superficial. The localization of alienation in the structures of capitalist society has led to a 'messianic crisis', for history's enigma cannot be resolved by history itself and to change man's working conditions does not affect his internal tensions.

(c) The priority of praxis over theory is impossible, because transforming praxis is ultimately dependent upon 'conceptual patterns, which extend beyond experience and beyond the success of the practical attempts' (in Marx's case the utopia of 'total' man).[12]

Moltmann believes that these 'errors' in Marxist theory inevitably lead to either disillusionment or terrorism (or both). In the latter case, action is directed exclusively to the conquering of political power. Such a goal springs from a closed and basically irrational system of thought which makes freedom dependent upon the acceptance of only one legitimate praxis. It is bound to give rise to a conservative use of power, capable only of destroying values and institutions to which it is negatively related.[13]

Building on his understanding of the God of biblical revelation, and in dialogue with Marxist political theory, Moltmann elaborates a 'political theology' which aims at forging a new liberating praxis for the church.

Theology must begin with the God of the exodus, for only this God calls his people out of bondage, not from the material world into a spiritual one, but from all present oppression into the future of liberty. Freedom begins when we experience history as a movement between exodus and arrival, between promise and fulfilment. The exodus shows us that history is not neutral. Rather, it is the history of mankind's presumption, despair, alienation and rejection of God's purposes. The resulting future of oppression and repression culminated in the crucifixion of Jesus Christ.

Moltmann sees the cross in dialectical terms.[14] On the one hand, it is the culminating revelation of man's true alienation and the

---

[12] *Ibid.*, pp. 47–59.   [13] *Ibid.*, pp. 96–104.

[14] His second major work, *The Crucified God: the Cross of Christ as the Foundation and Criticism of Christian Theology* (London, 1974) is a major exposition of the meaning of the cross for theology and for our generation. He sees it as complementing his *Theology of Hope*: 'The dominant theme then was that of *anticipations* of the future of God in the form of promises and

negation of the accumulated misery of each generation. On the other hand, it achieves reconciliation by opening up a future when love will be free of all anguish and paternalism. Only the cross as the consummation of mankind's historical estrangement, complemented by the resurrection, can make possible a history freed from every kind of tyranny.[15]

In the light of the depths of desolation, despair and foresakenness revealed in the crucified God, the question of mankind's historical alienation cannot be reduced to his mere social existence. Man is also ontologically self-alienated, confronted with the universality and finality of death. Death does not allow man to escape easily from the source of his alienation. However, the resurrection of the abandoned Messiah removes the ultimate terror of death.

Contrary to the Marxist view, Christian faith is neither 'the existence of a defect', nor 'an inverted world.' Firstly, the crucifixion, by denying to sin and death an eternal reality, rejects the factuality of what already exists. Secondly, the resurrection makes possible already within the oppression of the old order that new freedom without which no genuine transformation of structures can take place.

The church is challenged both by ideological criticism and by the more radical criticism of the cross to adopt a new liberating praxis.

Firstly, its theological thinking needs to be transformed. Theology is not a neutral search for truth but part of an historical criticism which leads to the transformation of society.[16]

Secondly, it should support that style of democracy which springs from the rejection of the idolatry of absolute power.[17] This will

---

hopes; here it is the understanding of the *incarnation* of that future, by way of the sufferings of Christ, in the world's sufferings. Moving away from Ernst Bloch's philosophy of hope, I now turn to the questions of 'negative dialectic' and the 'critical theory' of T. W. Adorno and M. Horkheimer . . . This theology of the cross . . . is intended to make the theology of hope more concrete, and to add the necessary power of resistance to the power of its visions to inspire to action' (p. 5).   [15] 'Liberation in the Light of Hope', p. 418.

[16] *Cf.* Moltmann's essay in *Kirche im Prozess der Aufklärung* (Munich, 1970) and his Carnahan lectures in Buenos Aires (1977), *Temas para una teologia de la esperanza* (Buenos Aires, 1978).

[17] In 'Religion, Revolution and Future', Moltmann mentions three basic abuses of power: *economic* – hunger is due to economic exploitation; *political* – self-determination for some people is made impossible by the vested interests of the élite of the imperialist nations; and *racial* – white man's progress has been achieved by the retrogression of the black. Also, compare his identification of five basic areas where liberation must be won today, in 'Liberation in the Light of Hope', pp. 426–428.

imply a struggle against all one-party systems in which man's nature and future are determined by an all-embracing ideology, and for an 'open society' in which genuine liberties are tenaciously defended and the possibility of constant structural change guaranteed.[18]

Thirdly, its commitment to the cross in preaching and life should aim at converting modern man from his twin illusions of success and power, into a being capable of *sym-pathia* (suffering alongside) and joy, a man free from all anxieties.[19]

The main significance of Moltmann's approach to a theology of the 'political liberation of mankind'[20] is his attempt to set the total meaning of the Christ event within the framework of a future, universal eschatology:

> We must try once again to read history eschatologically with a 'reversed sense of time' and return from the future of Christ to his past. In terms of history and its sense of time, Jesus first died and was then raised. In eschatological terms the last becomes the first: he died as the risen Christ and was made flesh as the one who was to come.[21]

This seems to me to be basically a valid procedure, particularly when, as for Moltmann, the eschatological coming Kingdom is a concrete reality. God's final and complete liberation of man from

> the prison of sin, law and death . . . calls for something to correspond to it in political life, so that liberations from the prisons of capitalism, racism and technocracy must be understood as parables of the freedom of faith.[22]

Though I accept that eschatology gives us a solid framework for discovering God's demands for change in society today, I am not satisfied that Moltmann has really grasped the nettle: the relationship

---

[18] In 'On Latin American Liberation Theology: An Open Letter to José Miguez Bonino', *Christianity and Crisis*, 36, 29 March 1976, pp. 57–63, Moltmann argues vigorously for democratic socialism which he believes will guarantee both civil liberties and economic liberation. He is wary of all theoretical arguments for a socialist dictatorship, however transitory it is meant to be, for there has been no evidence yet of socialisms moving towards democracy.

[19] *Cf.* J. Moltmann, *Theology and Joy* (London, 1973), especially chapter 5: 'The Liberating Church a Testing Ground of the Kingdom of God.'

[20] The title of chapter 8 of *The Crucified God*.   [21] *Ibid.*, p. 184.   [22] *Ibid.*, pp. 319–320.

between the eschatological liberation, which includes the groaning creation, and the personal justification of the individual who accepts that in Christ's death his sin has been borne and his guilt removed. Moltmann views the cross essentially in terms of a theodicy: whether there is a righteous God who ultimately vindicates justice and reconciliation against 'the cries for righteousness of those who are murdered and gassed, who are hungry and oppressed.'[23] The cross answers this question affirmatively because it displays God both suffering and overcoming historical human alienation. Moltmann does acknowledge that God's righteousness is available for the believer in the overcoming of his guilt, but he does not show sufficiently clearly how this is to be appropriated. Perhaps, for fear of succumbing again to the Western churches' strong temptation to adopt an individualist faith and ethic, Moltmann does not distinguish too clearly between the special community of the redeemed, who experience at first-hand Christ's power to produce a new kind of existence, and the rest of humanity who may expect some kind of benefit from Christ's eschatological victory over the idolatries of power, race and economic privilege.

Johann-Baptist Metz

Like Moltmann, Metz takes seriously the context for theology of post-war Germany: a society which, after the catastrophe of the Third Reich, has discovered an unexpected pluralism and which is repelled in practice but fascinated in theory by Marxism. Both seek to rescue theology from the individualistic morass of existentialism, and to turn it into a critical, disciplined analysis of trends in society in dialogue with current utopias.[24]

There are, however, differences of emphasis. Metz sees theology more in terms of a dialogue between the church's traditions and the modern world, whose purpose is mutual criticism and correction. He is particularly concerned with the political implications of the deceleration of the Catholic Church's post-Vatican reformation, due, he believes, to a certain panic in the face of a new freedom.[25] Unlike

---

[23] *Ibid.*, p. 175.

[24] *Cf.* 'L'église et le monde' in *Théologie d'aujourd'hui et demain* (Paris, 1967), p. 153.

[25] *Cf.* J. B. Metz, 'Does the Church need a new Reformation?', *Conc.* VI, 2, 1970; 'Freiheit als philosphische-theologische Grenzproblem' in *Gott im Welt: Festgabe für Karl Rahner* (Freibourg, 1964).

Moltmann, he does not really attempt to supply a solid biblical basis for his political theology.

Metz sets forth his most systematic thinking in *Theologie der Welt*,[26] in which he debates three crucial problems: the world, the task of theology, and the responsibility of the church in the modern world.

The world

Theology should be aware that the modern world, partly as the result of the Christian faith's sustained attack on the primitive mythical view of nature, has irrevocably embraced the secularist ideal.

Secularization is characterized by:

(a) *Pluralism.* Modern man has rejected the claim made by any one world-view to possess an exclusive understanding of reality.

(b) *Openness to the future.* The object of faith is no longer a world beyond history but a new world beyond the present which man himself is capable of constructing. Man is absorbed in planning for a better world.

(c) *Pragmatism.* Man bases his reasoning more on practical experience than on intellectual reflection. The advent of technology, some believe, has made all ideologies superfluous.

(d) *Post-atheism.* Religious belief has been relegated to the private sector of man's life. Secularized society no longer engages in antireligious polemic, for God does not enter into the calculations of functionalist planning.

Metz believes that the church ought to accept much of this process, not because it is a *fait accompli*, but because it corresponds to a Christian understanding of the world.

This understanding springs from the doctrines of creation and incarnation. God has manifested himself in the world as the instigator and dynamic principle of history. He is not, therefore, the object of a metaphysical and atemporal faith, but Immanuel. Transcendence has been converted into event. History is real, for God has accepted the world in his Son. What God has accepted he will not, like other gods, either violate, absorb or divinize. He has created the world distinct from himself by a free act, and as a free gift. Therefore, he does not have to enter into competition with the world, rather he

[26] Mainz, 1968.

guarantees its 'otherness', its non-divinity. He frees it from a cosmic-centredness, based on a nature pantheism, and makes it man-centred in order that it may fulfil his purpose. God's acceptance of his creation means that he is free to be Lord of all and man is free to unloose creation's latent possibilities.

Nevertheless, only a naïve person would fail to see that secularization is an ambiguous and contradictory process. The Christian understanding of history is conditioned by the sign of the cross, the permanent symbol of the world's protest against God. The doctrines of creation and incarnation can never be divorced in Christian thinking from the doctrines of sin and salvation. Secularization demonstrates both acceptance and contradiction.

However, the contradictions do not vitiate the process itself; rather they demonstrate the need to eradicate its deviations and flaws, for secularization exposes the dangers of freedom in a technological era. Man is not threatened by secularization as such, but by the false gods and ideologies which betray it.[27] Man, therefore, is not called to separate himself from the world, only to renounce the present world whenever it is seduced by its own prestige and power.

The task of theology

(a) *Dialogue.* Metz is concerned with the interaction between the secular world and theology. Theology's task is not to dispute with other theologies over meanings but to engage in the debate about the society of the future. In order to bring together contemporary utopias and the Christian promise of universal peace and justice, theology should think eschatologically. An eschatological theology becomes a 'political theology' when it assumes the responsibility of constructively criticizing the world's social reality.

Only when theology has made genuine contact with society can it contribute something unique from its own eschatological perspective. Christian eschatological theology, because it takes seriously man's alienation – his sense of guilt and evil – and because it denies that mere economic transformation can solve this problem, is a 'negative theology of the future.'[28] As such it radically questions the

[27] Metz includes Marxism among the false ideologies because it has identified 'hominization' of the world with autonomous humanization, *i.e,* eschatological self-liberation.

[28] *Cf.* 'Responsabilidad de la esperanza' in J. Aguirre *et al., Los problemas de un diálogo* (Madrid, 1969), pp. 152–153.

militant optimism of certain future-orientated ideologies.

(b) *In search of a praxis*. Like Moltmann, Metz considers that theology needs to be thoroughly transformed, partly because it often acts ideologically (*e.g.* when it justifies the secular ambition or economic privileges of the church), and partly because it has largely failed to grapple with society's social problems.[29]

In the first case theology is in constant danger of surrendering to the pressures of modern socio-political ideologies. In the second case, the Christian message is not reaching modern man, because it has removed him from his social and political context. As the early church did not make Jesus into a private object of worship, but acknowledged him to be the Lord of the universe and thus in conflict with the existing political order, so today we cannot confine the biblical promises of liberty, justice, peace and reconciliation to a private religious world, but must apply them critically to all existing circumstances.

Theology will be transformed when we adopt an adequate 'political hermeneutic'. This hermeneutic is founded on God's promise, grounded in his covenant with his people (for whom, for the first time, the world appears as history), and orientated towards the future. This area of promise makes the biblical message into a powerful, contemporary, critical and liberating force for the ideological and political commitments of both church and world.

The different perspectives of the biblical and the modern worlds can be brought together (the task of hermeneutics) because the modern world's openness to the future is guaranteed by the biblical belief in the promise. They are brought together by what Metz describes as 'the dangerous memory', *i.e.* the memory of the liberating power inherent in Jesus' subversive attitudes and actions on behalf of the weak against the powerful.[30]

The search for a political hermeneutic is an attempt to find a new Christian language which will transform man's existing consciousness, based on the triviality of things as they are, into one which is critically orientated to an uncharted future. The authenticity of this

---

[29] *Cf.* 'Los problemas de la iglesia después del concilio' in K. Rahner, *et al.*, *La respuesta de los teólogos* (Buenos Aires, 1970), pp. 168–170; 172–174 and 'In place of an editorial', *Conc.*, VII, 2, 1971.

[30] *Cf.* 'The Future in the Light of the Memory of the Passion', *Conc.*, VIII, 1972, pp. 317ff.

hermeneutic will be proved by its danger to existing structures and its power to convert love into situations of real liberation.

The church's responsibility

Metz's final concern is to see the church transformed into a critical and liberating force within society.

He suggests that the church's liberating praxis will involve accepting the reality of secularization, while opposing its tendency to convert freedoms into idolatries. It will also mean that the church must offer its skills for the construction of an eschatological order of justice, humanization and universal peace.

The church will approach its responsibility without any illusions about the alienating and idolatric powers loose in the secular situation. The world's fundamental problem is that it cannot take its own secular process with sufficient seriousness; it is, therefore, ever looking for new myths and ideologies. In other words, instead of assuming full responsibility for the future, mankind turns its historical moment into a new profane religion which enslaves rather than liberates.

In the light of this trend, the church should seek to fulfil the following tasks of social criticism:

(a) Protect the individual against abstract concepts of progress,[31] for the value of individuality cannot be quantified in relation to human progress.

(b) Oppose all tendencies to absolute power in both state and church, for no one agency in the world can in itself be the complete subject of history.

(c) manifest the difference between a dogmatic approach to sociological analysis and social criticism.

(d) While generally supporting a planned future, protest against identifying it with ends set by technology alone.

To be a liberating force in today's closed world, the church must pay close attention to the biblical message of liberty. This

at one and the same time frees man from the chains of sin and death through Christ crucified and also affirms man's liberation . . . from every

---

[31] Metz maintains that the main difference between Christian and secular eschatology is the former's comparative ignorance of the future, cf. 'L'église et le monde', p. 154.

historical force and every human absolutization and self-enthronement
. . . It is an emancipating force, because it demystifies and relativises
every power and every lordship and returns our responsibility to us, thus
inaugurating the human history of freedom.[32]

The church's task is to be 'the institutionalised interest of this freedom',[33] while the task of a political theology is to make the church
aware of its liberating function in society.

Though writing at the end of the 1960s, before a substantial reaction had set in against the optimistic accounts of the secularization
process by men like Harvey Cox, Metz does succeed in giving a
relatively balanced account of its positive and negative facets. But a
serious weakness remains in his attempt to provide a theological
assessment of this process and to offer guidelines for the church's
future involvement in a secular society; for he fails to propose any
solution to an inherent contradiction at the very heart of the process.

According to his analysis, secularization arose as a logical response
to the Christian faith's success in demythologizing the forces and
structures of nature. Put the other way round, it is probably true to
say that without the sanction of the Christian view of the world the
whole process of modernization would not have taken place. Now,
however, the process has become almost completely divorced from
Christian values, some of which would have helped to turn it in a
different, more humane, direction. This subsequent divergence arose
partly because the churches allowed the ideology of secularism to
dictate the terms of a truce in which the gospel was to be interpreted
in individualistic and private terms, concerned almost exclusively
with a right relationship to God, and with worship, prayer and
personal ethics.

Today the secularization process as an ideology is gaining far fewer
converts, and some of its fundamental ideals are being seriously
questioned. Fear of exploitation and control through highly sophisticated technological devices, and grave doubts about the possibility
of continuous economic growth, because of its very serious inherent
side-effects as well as obvious defects in the classical explanations of
current crises in the economic order, have led many people to seek

---

[32] Quote taken from his article in the symposium, *Kirsche im Prozess der Aufklärung*, entitled,
'Ecclesiastical Authority in the Face of the History of Freedom.'

again some kind of world-view which would help guide humanity into an uncertain future. An increasing number of educated people are choosing Marxism, not necessarily because of the rigour of its analysis of historical forces in society today (in a number of respects it is still living on the borrowed insights of the past), but because it offers a cause worth struggling for compared with what appears to be the senile indifference and superficiality of much contemporary Western culture.

The contradiction lies in the fact that secularization, built on the biblical view of the relationship between God, man and nature, has bitten the hand which originally fed it. Solutions to the present crisis are sought everywhere but in the Christian world-view. Secularization, far from ending ideologies, seems likely to spawn an even greater variety of them, as its own contradictions become increasingly more difficult to live with – not least the spiralling effect of technological and bureaucratic complexity.

Metz is aware of the tensions in modern, post-industrial society and believes that the church should be involved in helping to shape a human future based on Christian principles. However, he does not tell us how this might become a reality while the Western churches continue to be dominated by two basic options: either by a type of evangelism which fails to take socio-political issues seriously, or by social action divorced from the belief that all people without a saving knowledge of the biblical Christ are lost for ever. What the churches of the West need is a greater theological revolution than Metz imagines, one which liberates their leaders to exercise a constructive prophetic ministry. This revolution will come about when Christians manage to bring together in theory and in practice the biblical understanding of man and contemporary insights into the historical forces which have shaped his present society.

Helmut Gollwitzer

Paul Oestreicher has done us the great service of describing those particular circumstances in Gollwitzer's life which have shaped his theology.[34] A member of the German Confessing Church, he became

---

[33] *Ibid.*

[34] 'H. Gollwitzer in the European Storms' in H. Gollwitzer, *The Demands of Freedom: Papers by a Christian in West Germany* (London, 1965), pp. 7–27.

the pastor of Niemöller's church in Berlin when the latter was arrested in 1940. Later he was drafted into the German army and in 1945 was captured by the Russians and held prisoner for four years.[35]

His personal experiences have deeply influenced both his style of doing theology and its subject-matter. Oestreicher comments that his involvement in a preaching and pastoral ministry is unusual in German academic circles, and that by committing himself politically against the establishment he has frequently risked his academic reputation: 'the Kirchenkampf (church struggle) had taught him the need to preach the immediate relevance of the Kingdom to the political and economic life of man.'[36]

Gollwitzer seeks to think theologically out of, and in the service of, concrete historical situations. In this respect, together with men like Niemöller and Thielicke who were likewise involved in the struggle against Nazism, he marks a more definite break with postwar German individualistic, existentialist and socially uninvolved theology than do men of the younger generation like Moltmann.[37]

His own personal experience of Communism as well as his concern for peace in a divided Germany compelled Gollwitzer to take seriously the challenge of Marxism to contemporary theology. Involved in the Christian-Marxist encounter, he has reflected deeply on the importance of the Marxist criticism of religion,[38] on the social implications of the gospel and on the revolutionary nature of the Christian church as a new community.

With regard to Marxism, Gollwitzer starts by clarifying the distinction between Marx and Lenin. When Marx's prophetic prediction of the spontaneous rising of the European proletariat to inaugurate a new world-order was not fulfilled, Lenin deliberately and violently redirected the course of history towards preselected goals. Instead of relying on the automatic evolution of a dialectical process, he based his strategy on an unrestricted will-to-power and an ascetic devotion to a 'messianic' ideal.[39]

Leninist Communism transformed Marxism from a total revol-

---

[35] His experiences and reflections of this period are set forth in *Unwilling Journey: a Diary from Russia* (London, 1953).

[36] *The Demands of Freedom*, p. 11.   [37] *Ibid.*, pp. 50, 53, 145.

[38] H. Gollwitzer, *The Marxist Criticism of Religion and the Christian Faith* (London, 1967).

[39] *The Demands of Freedom*, pp. 99–100.

utionary theory into an ideological justification of the seizure of power in one nation. All it now offers, in a pseudo-scientific guise, is a simple sort of humanism, a salvation from nihilism and pessimism and the promise of the satisfaction of all material needs.[40]

From the perspective of authentic Christian faith, the Marxist charge that religion is a symptom of an alienated existence, rather than the nucleus of human life itself, is very superficial. Claiming that religion is only of secondary importance, Marxism presents itself as the fulfilment of man's primary needs.[41] As a result it poses itself as a substitute, immanent religion of a new world, in which a transcendent God is replaced by a transcendent hope in a future always open to new possibilities for man.[42]

Marxism, in spite of its messianic pretensions and its failure to account for certain historical trends,[43] has forced theology to face the church's own notable failures and compromises.

Too often the church has been used by the dominant segments of society to eliminate any real challenge from below to its power, privileges and prestige by inculcating interest in personal happiness and holiness in the future as the real province of salvation, and by presenting the world as a sphere in the grip of immutable and irremovable forces. Its tendency ever since 'the victory of paganism over Christianity' in the post-Constantinian period has been to preach a fatalistic submission of the believer to whatever the current ruling classes have deemed expedient.[44]

Whenever the church has succumbed to this temptation it has, according to Gollwitzer, betrayed the revolutionary stance implied in Jesus' announcement of the Kingdom as the new order where all power structures and property relations will be transformed, the institution of slavery and the practice of racism abolished and all inflexible conduct predicated on human law eliminated.[45] To live

---

[40] Ibid., pp. 105, 145ff.

[41] The Marxist Criticism of Religion, pp. 16–21, 177–179.

[42] 'Ernst Bloch's Atheistic Interpretation of what the Bible Says of God' in H. Gollwitzer, The Existence of God as Confessed by Faith (London, 1965), pp. 97–98.

[43] At the beginning of 1977 Pravda carried an article in which it admitted that the anti-religious educational crusade among the youth in Russia was not bearing the fruit hoped for. Now was the time to inculcate vigorously 'a dialectic and materialist organic view of the world' (my italics), report in La Opinión (Buenos Aires, 6 April 1977).

[44] 'Liberation in History', Int. 28 October 1974, p. 419; The Marxist Criticism of Religion, pp. 183–184.   [45] Ibid., pp. 411ff.

according to the way of the Kingdom will mean forming subversive groups which are both enemies of the old world and witnesses of a new.[46]

Gollwitzer opposes the idea, on theological and historical grounds, that the preaching of the gospel is concerned primarily with the revolution of hearts from which a revolution of structures will automatically follow. He believes this idea is a bourgeois illusion and counter-revolutionary.[47] On the contrary, if the reality of the new order is present in the Christian community it must overflow the borders of that community into society. Taking issue with Conzelmann's exegesis of Colossians 3:11, he says that new life in Christ is not simply a matter of 'invalidating inner-worldly differences within the Church, but the privileges and disadvantages resulting from them.' The firm separation of two realms – one within the church where, theoretically, equality would reign, and another outside where Christian brethren could continue to experience substantial differences in the quality and availability of health care and educational opportunities – is inconceivable.[48]

If inequality in the world is largely due, as Gollwitzer believes, to a class struggle promoted from above,[49] then the church, because of its commitment to the new age in Christ, should support those socialist movements which promote real democracy and freedom:

> If in socialism the issue is to transform society into a free, brotherly and solidary society with no dominant rulers, overcoming a society based on privilege, because of scarcity, then the model of primitive Christianity implies a tendency towards socialism, disagreement with class society and opposition to feudal and bourgeois ways of life.[50]

However, support for socialism does not imply commitment to

---

[46] *Ibid.*, p. 411.

[47] 'Die gesellschaftlichen Implikationen des Evangeliums' in K. Herbert, *et al.*, *Christliche Freiheit im Dienst am Menschen* (Frankfurt, 1972), p. 146.

[48] 'Liberation in History', p. 416.

[49] He gives as one example the 1973 military *coup* in Chile: 'the class struggle of the privileged is resolutely prepared to commit any brutality whenever they are not able to guarantee their rule. . . Capitalism of necessity resorts to violence when its position is endangered.' 'Learning from Chile', *Christianity and Crisis*, 34, 1974, p. 99.

[50] 'Die gesellschaftlichen Implikationen des Evangeliums', p. 152; 'Learning from Chile', p. 100.

any secular messianism or to the utopian illusions of dogmatic social-ist movements, but is the response of Christian freedom to the demands of the gospel in the wider community of the world. Goll-witzer is not naïve. He recognizes that an external situation of liberty does not necessarily create free men, and that new slaveries are very possible even in situations of freedom.

The main point at issue is that the church should proclaim a gospel addressed primarily to the oppressed, revoking for ever its alliance with the rulers of the old age.

Like Moltmann, Gollwitzer has decidedly rejected in practice the traditional two-kingdom model of the relationship between church and state. He would argue, then, that Romans 13:1–7 cannot be pressed to mean that the church has no responsibility to declare the implications of the gospel for the state. If all political power and policies are ultimately accountable to the God of the nations, the churches, as stewards of the gospel, have a duty to spell this out in particular circumstances without, of course, becoming political agents themselves.

But we still await from Gollwitzer a thoroughgoing exposition of the way organized Christian faith (the institutional churches) can witness to the essentially political nature of its message without falling again into the trap of identifying its own future with particular political or social forces.

Within evangelical Protestantism today there are three main tend-encies, all of which claim to be the responsible biblical approach to Christian social involvement: first, the Calvinist tradition, associated with men like Kuyper and Dooyeweerd, which emphasizes the call of the church to 'Christianize' secular institutions in line with a biblical understanding of man; second, the pietist tradition, which has given precedence to personal regeneration as the prior require-ment before social structures can be meaningfully changed; and third, the radical reformed tradition which concentrates on the renewal of the Christian community as an alternative society, and which, living in a completely different way from the standards accepted by society at large, aims to preach both the hope and the judgment of the gospel.

Gollwitzer combines some aspects of all these elements in his thinking, but not in a way which adds up to a creative synthesis of their more relevant insights. Such a synthesis would demand both tenacious thinking and sacrificial living, and is probably some way off. The faithfulness and authenticity of contemporary witness to the truth of the gospel may well depend upon a persistent struggle to achieve it in both word and deed.

Chapter Five

Eastern Europe:
practical Marxism and dogmatic atheism

The difficulties and dangers of living in a socialist society are only overcome by a profound understanding of the Gospel, inward rebirth, real fellowship in repentance love, hope and faith, an adequate, fearless, courageous understanding of historical changes, and by priestly compassion for men living close to us. There is nothing more glorious, fascinating, overwhelming and creative than the Gospel of the living Lord in the midst of toiling, rebellious, suffering and struggling humanity.

J. L. Hromadka, 'Biblical Theology in the Ecumenical Struggle' in R. C. Mackie and C. C. West, *Essays on the Ecumenical Hope* (1963).

In the years immediately following World War II Europe witnessed a remarkable shift in the ideological balance of power. By the end of the 1940s, Leninist Marxism was firmly established in nearly a dozen nations east of a line drawn from Kiel to Vienna and Trieste.

Those churches of Jesus Christ which found themselves, by force of circumstances, to the east of this imaginary line, were confronted by a political situation so dramatically different from what they had experienced before that they had to reconsider almost from scratch the relevance of the gospel to this new phenomenon.

The complete history of this process of readjustment has not yet been written. We intend to focus on one small fragment of it in order to demonstrate how two church members have grappled theologically with the challenge of conducting the life of their church in an officially and militantly atheistic secular society. The two men, both Czechs, are Josef Hromadka (1889–1969) and Jan Milich Lochman.[1] They have been chosen because they represent the most self-

---

[1] Lochman no longer resides in Czechoslovakia. He now teaches theology in Basle, Switzerland.

conscious and systematic new theological approach to revolution coming from behind the Iron Curtain.

At the time of the swift transition of their society to a monochrome socialist system, they were faced with a momentous choice which was to guide their theological steps for the next twenty years. Either they would fit into an apologetic role, such as certain church leaders from the West assigned to them, defending the cold-war definition of democratic freedom,[2] or else they had to reassess the church's mission from within the system, resisting pressures, however well-intentioned, from without. They chose the latter course and thus gave to the universal church a new perspective on how to relate the gospel to a substantially new social situation.

The challenge caused them to search for reliable theological guidelines which would enable them to respond creatively to the church's particular vocation at that time. They found these guidelines firstly in a thorough re-evaluation of the church's real position in a post-Christian Europe, secondly in a fresh discovery of their particular Reformation heritage, and thirdly in the use of a theological methodology which related the biblical reality of God's new order in Christ to the daily experiences of a minority community in a hostile environment.

From the perspective of a church divested of all special privileges in society, Hromadka and Lochman were able to perceive with startling clarity the effective end of the *Corpus Christianum* in Europe. Through a sober and honest analysis of the characteristics of the post-Constantinian church, they came to the conclusion that the decay of evangelical fervour among European churches is the inevitable effect of a policy which has generally refused, for centuries, to count the cost of a prophetic admonition of the ruling powers. By the mid-20th century, the church's failure to question fundamental aspects of the development of Western civilization had overtaken it. The salt had lost its savour, because the church had all too readily identified itself with those who had always felt threatened by the conduct and message of its Saviour.

A candid appraisal of the church's present reality should lead firstly to a thorough reassessment of the church's past relationship

---

[2] *Cf.* Lochman, 'The Lordship of Christ in a Secularized World' in *LW*, 14, 1967, p. 74.

to given societies. By emphasizing harmony and stability and by adopting a fatalistic approach to divine providence the church has almost unremittingly supported the existing order.[3] Lochman thinks this is partly because the Lordship of Christ has been understood within a cosmological rather than an eschatological framework. Christ is viewed as a celestial monarch, dispensing an unquestionable and abstract justice like an oriental tyrant, and maintaining a certain inner cohesion in society against disintegrating pressures from the 'godless' outside. In etymological terms Christ is depicted as a *despotēs*, not as the New Testament *kyrios* who has vanquished all those authorities who claim to exercise a power in any way independent of his universal sovereignty. The cosmological Christ, portrayed as a heavenly Charlemagne, upholding and extending Christian civilization, has served as a foundation and ideology for the whole disreputable church tradition of caesaropapism which, even in our days, has rationalized a hierarchically structured and unequal society.[4] This way of looking at Christianity and society is finished. As Hromadka says, there 'can be no way back'.[5]

The second important conclusion to be drawn from the new situation is that radical changes taking place in East European society represent an invitation to the church, both in the East and the West, to reconsider its theological perspectives. The church in the East should be careful not to measure the presence or absence of divine favour by the Western pattern of bourgeois democracy; the church in the West should be prepared to ask itself whether certain aspects of a socialist society do not represent the social consequences of the gospel more faithfully than the liberal democracies of the so-called 'free world'.[6]

New situations always create new opportunities for the church, as long as it does not react to changes in a pharisaical and moralistic fashion. The church is challenged to reconsider courageously its theological presuppositions. Hromadka and Lochman do this by seeking to re-establish in changed circumstances those theological fundamentals which will stimulate the church to a fresh *reformatio:*

---

[3] *Ibid.*, p. 74.   [4] *Ibid.*, pp. 69–71.

[5] *Theology between Yesterday and Tomorrow* (Philadelphia, 1957), p. 65.

[6] *Ibid.*, pp. 63–64, 75; Article in *Zürcher Woche* (19 January 1962), reprinted in H. Gollwitzer, *The Demands of Freedom; Papers by a Christian in West Germany* (London, 1965), pp. 151–156.

'wrestling for an evangelical obedience that encompasses all of life.'[7]

Fortunately for them and for us, a confrontation between the gospel and revolutionary change was not a totally new experience in the history of their church. Both of them repeatedly refer to the theological and political heritage which stems from the radical Reformation of John Huss and the Bohemian Brethren.

Two aspects of this heritage are particularly relevant to the kind of situation in which the church finds itself in a Marxist society. In the first place, the church of the Czech Reformation deliberately renounced all power alliances with the state. Seeking to apply its rediscovery of the radical nature of the biblical message – namely the reality of God's acts of liberation on behalf of the despised and oppressed, releasing them from the primeval curse of sin and death and from the power of malignant forces[8] – the church accepted its role as a minority group in society, dependent only upon the power of the gospel to produce change. The acceptance of this role implied that the church would practise a consistent, radical discipleship

> rejecting participation . . . in earthly power, compulsion, vengeance, self-defense and war; proclaiming the commandment of compassion, forgiveness, love as the only mark of discipleship and membership of the Church, never forgetting the invisible but real line between the Church and the world.[9]

With this background in mind the church, in the years following the Communist take-over, was able to adjust more readily to the removal of its privileges and to the harassment it received from party officials.

In the second place, this church of the 'first' Reformation (the break with medieval Christianity in Czechoslovakia) did not withdraw from all involvement in social and political affairs on account of its non-participation in power.[10] It rejected the kind of dualism which was later to become embodied in the much-discussed Lutheran doctrine of the two kingdoms, confronting the world with the need

---

[7] 'The Lordship of Christ in a Secularized World', *op. cit.*, p. 66.

[8] J. M. Lochman, 'Importance of Theology for Church and Society', *SJT*, 26, 1973, p. 263.

[9] *Theology between Yesterday and Tomorrow*, pp. 93–94.

[10] Lochman, 'The Church and the Humanization of Society', *USQR*, 24, 1969, p. 134.

to purify its systems in the light of the eschatological Kingdom of Christ. The Czech reformers' favourite metaphor for the church was the *communio viatorum*, the company of those who were never completely at home in any given culture or social system.[11] In particular, they emphasized the eternal call to freedom and justice within society.

Clearly, with this strongly prophetic and critical strand in its theological roots, the church had no reason to be perturbed by dramatic structural changes even when, after 1945, these threatened its very existence. As the church had once disengaged itself from the remnants of feudalism, so it could relinquish whatever crumbs might have fallen its way from the table of a liberal bourgeois society.[12]

Nevertheless, paradoxically, it is precisely these two aspects of its heritage which have enabled the church to come to terms with revolutionary changes, which have also caused it to view them with a certain critical detachment. Hromadka's attitude to the socialist revolution was less critical than that of Lochman. He started from the assumption, already discussed, that the changes were irrevocable and many of them urgently necessary.[13] He believed that certain points of Marxist thought should prove fertile ground for theological reflection: particularly the linking of theory with practical life; the emphasis on historical conditioning in the development of political theory; the relating of human freedom to social justice for the whole community and the striving after change which would result in a more equal and fraternal society for all. At the same time he clearly sees the dangers inherent in the Marxist programme: for example, the danger of interpreting humanity as just one part of some superior, impersonal process of nature and history, and of self-deception in the predicting of a social order capable of solving all material, moral and spiritual problems. The message of the Scriptures transcends

[11] J. L. Hromadka, 'Approche évangélique de l'homme', *ETR*, 47, 1972, pp. 30–31.

[12] For a comment on Hromadka's positive, yet critical, acceptance of the reality of change in his country and its background in the Czech Reformation, *cf.* E. V. Kohak, 'Theology behind the Iron Curtain: a Challenge and a Reply,' *Encounter*, 26, 1965, pp. 362–372.

[13] Hromadka's disillusionment with Western liberal democracy and his espousal of some form of socialism antedates his actual experience of a Marxist society: the transition period occurred towards the latter half of the 1930s, *cf.* J. C. Bennett, 'Josef Hromadka: 1889–1969', *Christianity and Crisis*, 30, 1970, pp. 20–22; E. A. Dowey, E. G. Homrighausen and C. C. West, 'Memorial: J. L. Hromadka' *PSB*, 63, 1970, pp. 77–80.

both nature and history as 'absolute' reference-points and contradicts any secular hope which pretends that man, on his own, can engineer a new heaven and a new earth.[14]

Hromadka, however, in the words of J. C. Bennett, was 'less than candid about the real state of affairs in the country during the Stalinist period.'[15]

Possibly because he was deeply convinced that Western society was incapable of fulfilling man's deepest aspirations, he overvalued the positive gains of the socialist revolution.[16] On the theoretical level he was somewhat naïve about Marxist atheism, believing it to be mainly a reaction to the 19th-century orthodox and liberal bourgeois God, rather than a fundamental theoretical presupposition of dialectal materialism.[17]

Like Christians elsewhere, Hromadka has relied too heavily, in his assessment of Communist society, on its utopian theoretical strain, accepting too readily at their face value the very far-reaching promises that are made in the name of revolution. In this way, I believe, he has been inclined to allow a certain Christian idealism to obscure the historical connection between the Marxist view of man as autonomous and 'divine', and the appalling and consistent failures of Marxist societies to respect man's inherent dignity as one who may not be manipulated by coercion and propaganda, however justifiable this might seem to be in terms of the rightness of particular political and economic systems.

Lochman's approach to the question of atheism is more profound and realistic. He sees it as a negative force for man, for though supposedly reflecting a desire for his liberation, it ends up by effectively denying his real humanity. Nevertheless, Lochman believes that the church should not make the fatal mistake of conducting a moralistic crusade against 'godless atheism'. Atheism is not an ultimate reality: it is basically only a reaction and, therefore, cannot create new beginnings. It is effectively demythologized by the gospel

---

[14] *Theology between Yesterday and Tomorrow*, pp. 70–77; *cf.* also Lochman, 'Christianity and Marxism: Convergence and Divergence', *Christianity and Crisis*, 29, 1969.

[15] *Theology between Yesterday and Tomorrow*, p. 22.

[16] *Cf.* 'The Present International Crisis', *Communio Viatorum*, XI, 1–2, 1968.

[17] J. L. Hromadka, *Gospel for Atheists* (I quote from the Spanish version, Montevideo, 1970), pp. 49–50; 'On the Threshold of Dialogue between Christians and Marxists', *Study Encounter* 1, 1965, p. 121.

which proclaims that God's saving work is objectively independent of any positive or negative response to it. Hence the Christian can free himself from the myth of atheism, in order to convince the atheist that he is much more than he thinks he is. He can then approach him with an 'inclusive gospel' in a spirit of humility and solidarity, eschewing the 'exclusive gospel' of a self-righteous 'excommunicative law'.[18]

This open and frank attitude towards atheists undoubtedly contributed to the fruitful Christian-Marxist dialogue, which was initiated by Hromadka and the Marxist philosopher Machovec, and which, in its turn, contributed notably to the 'Prague Spring' of 1968.

A sober realization of the church's underprivileged position in the new society and the rediscovery of the Czech Reformation's heritage of radical discipleship and freedom for God's future helped these men to discover a different method and task for theology from those apparent in Western Europe (at least until the mid-1960s).

Approaching the Bible along lines similar to those adopted by the German Confessing Church of the Hitler era, they sought to protect themselves against all temptations to view the message through the lenses of historically conditioned metaphysical systems. This meant that the church had to learn to evaluate any new historical situation unhurriedly and without recourse to prior dogmatic, ideological or national prejudices. It had to step outside the 'enslaving circle of (historical) analogies', so that the message of the gospel might be free to interpret and respond to historical events here and now.[19] This response would depend in part upon the careful use of certain tools developed by the social sciences to interpret man and his environment. The gospel frees us from fear of innovation and of new demands, and awakens in us a responsibility to find new ways to improve the world.[20]

Lochman believes that authentic theology can be carried out only by maintaining a continuous tension between the reality of a particular society as it confronts the church ('a theology which is no use in a concrete ecclesiastical or political community is a useless

---

[18] J. M. Lochman, 'Gospel for Atheists', *TT*, 26, 1969–70, pp. 301–308.

[19] J. L. Hromadka, *Gospel for Atheists*, pp. 81–83.

[20] J. L. Hromadka, 'On the Threshold', pp. 124–125.

theology') and the foundation documents of its particular confession ('the significance of theology is not ultimately decided pragmatically').

The tension is maintained in balance only when theology springs from a vital and engaged faith. Confession qualifies the subject matter of theology, namely God's eschatological involvement in human history; engaged confession qualifies the direction in which a theologian should develop his thought, namely the world in all its arrogance and greed to which God has come. The theme of God not only prohibits theology from retiring into 'the mighty fortress of transcendence' (as Ernst Bloch defined Karl Barth's theology of the Word), it demands its involvement in man's world, even exposing itself to the criticism of other disciplines.[21]

Costly theological reflection, in the midst of the pressures of a hostile and secular environment and a timid and pietistic church, led these men to a theological synthesis with ample practical consequences. The church must realize that Jesus Christ is not its property; that he does not automatically fight on its behalf, but also against it, and that he does not allow the church to possess the truth *over against* an unbelieving world, but rather *for* the world.[22] The church is called to forsake all its securities and many of its landmarks, in order to be able to plunge into the depths of other men's daily experiences. This does not mean, however, an uncritical acceptance of the claims and promises of new ideologies, for 'any effort to achieve a premature agreement or mutual assimilation can only lead to ideological confusion, ethical indecisiveness and practical inertia.'[23]

Lochman reminds us that the doctrine of justification is the *articulus aut stantis aut cadentis ecclesiae* not only in an individual sense, but also for the church's attitude towards, and action in, the world.[24] Justification counteracts ecclesiastical self-righteousness and liberates the church for true service (elsewhere called 'pro-existence' and 'diachronic christocracy'). This implies a costly identification with real people even when all natural and ideological sympathy stops.

[21] J. M. Lochman, 'Importance of Theology for Church and Society', pp. 258–261.
[22] J. L. Hromadka, 'Approche évangélique de l'homme', p. 28.
[23] J. L. Hromadka, 'On the Threshold', p. 124.
[24] J. M. Lochman, 'The Gospel and Social Action', *RW*, 32, 1973, pp. 347–348.

On the basis of justification, the Christian is called to turn uncon-ditionally towards all men. Such a stance distinguishes evangelical humanism from the current secular variety which 'loves boundaries too much.'[25]

Hromadka may never have envisaged the possibility that socialist societies could unleash such a nakedly aggressive and wholly unjus-tifiable repression as that suffered by the Czech people in August 1968.[26] Nevertheless, he was aware that unregenerate man would never be really free to produce a society which eliminated cynicism, apathy and fear of renewal. He was too defensive towards Western criticism of Communist society and too late in realizing that Soviet socialism, by its rigid opposition to the measures of freedom being won by Dubcek's 'socialism with a human face', proved that it represented no progress for humanity.[27]

Lochman, who has survived him, has always been more realistic about the possibility of substantial change inherent in the dynamic of human nature. He correctly sees that radical discipleship, such as inspired his forebears in the faith, is the only real driving force in attempts to reform the church and society: 'the demands of Jesus Christ are the signs of the eschatological existence which is possible and real under the Gospel regarding the imminent Kingdom of God.'[28]

---

[25] J. M. Lochman, 'The Lordship of Christ', pp. 77–78; 'Marxists' Expectations and Salvation in Christ', *CC*, 90, 1973, pp. 421–423.

[26] *Cf.* J. L. Hromadka 'On the Czech Invasion', *Christianity and Crisis*, 28, 1968, pp. 224–225.

[27] *Cf.* E. V. Kohak, 'Theology behind the Iron Curtain', pp. 370–372.

[28] J. M. Lochman, 'The Lordship of Christ', pp. 61, 75.

Chapter Six

White North America:
objections to the rich man's politics

After four years of resisting war, and many more years of resisting exploitation, misery and racism, we had taken thought among ourselves. Our conclusion: it was better to burn papers than to burn children.

Daniel Berrigan, *America is Hard to Find* (1973).

The continent of North America has produced two distinct approaches to the question of revolution and theology. As might be expected they arise from the different historical backgrounds of the white and black races.

In their respective criticisms of North American society there are points of agreement: both groups, for example, urge far-reaching changes in the system. Nevertheless, the daily experience of different skin colour has produced theologies whose agreements in content and methodology are often more formal than real.

Reflection on revolution among white theologians has grown and diversified within the last decade. There appear to be at least four main strands, though space will not allow us to treat each one separately. First, there is a group of theologians who have been influenced by the Christian-Marxist dialogue, Charles West, J. C. Bennett and Paul Lehmann among them. The second group comprises those who have reflected theologically out of active involvement in the anti-Vietnam War movement: its most famous representatives are the Berrigan brothers. Third, a number of theologians have more recently championed the concerns of Latin American Liberation Theology, seeking to apply them to the different social conditions of the USA. They include the group identified with the journal *Radical Religion*.[1] Fourth, there are those who have explored the theological significance for liberation of the feminist movement.[2]

The concerns of these four groups are not, of course, exclusive to any of them and there is a considerable overlap of interest, but they show the wide range covered by revolutionary theologies in the USA. We shall restrict ourselves here to considering a major theological treatise by the Protestant, Paul Lehmann, and to exploring the thought of the Roman Catholic priest and Jesuit, Daniel Berrigan.[3]

Paul Lehmann

Lehmann's major theological treatise on revolution[4] was planned initially as a response to the rejection of American society in the mid-1960s by large sectors of the black and student population. Later, it developed as a global treatment of revolution from a particular Christian perspective. The book's basic thesis is that

the pertinence of Jesus Christ to an age of revolution is the power of his presence to shape the passion for humanization that generated revolution, and thus preserve revolution from its own undoing.[5]

Lehmann deals with the question of revolution and theology on a broad canvas and in terms of theoretical possibilities. He believes that revolutions, because they release new principles of life into world history,[6] are desirable happenings. The new principles spring

---

[1] First published in 1974, *Radical Religion* is 'a quarterly journal whose main concern is scholarly investigation of the relationship between religion and social change.' Its commitment is to 'play an active role in political movements for liberation; to criticize economic injustice; to work for a socialist alternative; to explore the challenge of feminism to patriarchal religious systems; to discover our radical religious past through historical research; to examine the relationship between evangelical and politically active social Christianity; to study the controlling interests of our religious establishment; to understand how religion can be debilitating instead of liberating'. It is published in Berkeley, California.

[2] For example, Rosemary Radford Ruether, *New Woman, New Earth* (Seabury Press, 1975); Mary Daly, *Beyond God the Father* (Boston, 1973).

[3] Of the two brothers, Daniel has written more prolifically than Philip.

[4] P. Lehmann, *The Transfiguration of Politics: Jesus Christ and the Question of Revolution* (New York, 1974. London, 1975).   [5] *Ibid.*, p. xiii.   [6] *Ibid.*, p. 105.

from the criticism and transformation of privileged structures and regimes. Revolutions aim at making all life more human in a way that is possible only through the total destruction of all social systems which have become outmoded and dehumanizing.

However, all revolutions, without exception, have run into serious difficulties. Lehmann, in the main section of the book dedicated to examining revolutionary movements since World War II,[7] notes that no revolution has been able to fulfil adequately its promise of freedom and equality. The main cause of failure lies in an inadequate understanding of the dynamic reality and ambiguity of power, for revolutions 'are forced by the dynamics of their passions into a collision course with the stubborn radicality of good and evil in human affairs.'[8]

To create a new order, revolutionary movements have first to use force to overcome the inevitable resistance of the old order.

However, in practice, revolutions have mistaken their 'no' to the existing order for a new order, and thus have become self-justifying, self-righteous and self-perpetuating institutions. Ever since man's primal crime, the exercise of power as a result of the curse has invariably been divorced from the question of truth, so that, to legitimize its authority, it has had to appeal to its success. This has meant that no revolutionary group has been willing to admit that its own exercise of power can create a false consciousness, incapable of distinguishing between criticism from within the revolution and criticism of the revolution.[9]

The main task of revolutionary theology, Lehmann believes, is to help the revolution overcome the betrayal of its own principles. His starting-point is an investigation of the revolutionary life-style which

[7] Mao Tse Tung; Ho Chi Minh; Fidel Castro; Che Geuvara; Camilo Torres; Nestor Paz Zamora; Frantz Fanon; Martin Luther King; Malcolm X and the Black Panther Party. The revolutions concern the Far East, Latin America and the black population of the USA.

[8] *Ibid.*, p. 19.

[9] Currently, criticism of the petty and gross violation of human rights in Russia, Czechoslovakia and Poland is dismissed as anti-state propaganda. Such an admission, however, springs from that kind of tight nationalism which Marx criticized as part of a false consciousness. We may surmise that there is little difference between Hegel's defence of the Prussian state as the final incarnation of the unfolding universal 'Spirit' in the overcoming of the conflicts between all opposites, and the Soviet leaders' defence of the Russian state as the incarnation of a progressive socialist order. In both cases there is an uncritical acceptance of the *status quo* of a particular manifestation of power. In both cases history is paralysed.

Jesus Christ adopted in the face of the abuse of power he experienced.

Jesus Christ is an authentically revolutionary figure for he represents the model of a new humanity already present in the midst of the 'old age'. His revolutionary relevance to the ambiguity of power was demonstrated in his ministry and proved in the course of history. 'To the weakness of power Jesus juxtaposes the power of weakness. To the exercise of power . . . the refusal of power. To the pervasiveness of power . . . the transformation of power.'[10]

The power of weakness in Jesus' ministry is demonstrated first in his refusal of power and, second, in its transfiguration. As paradigms of this kind of power Lehmann picks out Paul's discussion of the Christian's response to the state (Rom. 13:1–7), and Jesus' confrontation of Pilate (Jn. 18 and 19). He argues that in neither case is the state's existence legitimized at all costs. Rather, both instances imply a radical questioning of particular power structures by methods which spring from the possibilities of a given situation and from the truth of the gospel.

Paul's main concern, Lehmann thinks, was to show how life in the new age should affect a Christian's relationship to the state. Although the Christian already enjoys life in the new age, he still has responsibilities in the old. Although he is called to a life-style of freedom from 'the pattern of this present world' (Rom. 12:2), this must not be interpreted as freedom for anarchy. So revolt against the powers established by God springs from self-righteous legalism, not from that love which is the fulfilling of the law. It implies the fanatical desire to impose the gospel on society as a new law. Just retribution belongs to God; he will repay. The true revolutionary attitude, therefore, is submission: firstly, because the authorities are already under God's judgment, for their use of violence proves that they are part of the logic of the old order; secondly, because Christians are to live out the demands of the new age, especially by serving their enemies.

> Thus, *submission* to existing authorities is *not* the confusion of obedience to God with the acceptance of the *status quo*. It is the confrontation of the weakness of power with the power of weakness. In this confrontation,

[10] *Ibid.*, p. 25.

the fear of retribution has been overruled by conscience, that is by the discernment that obedience to God and the practice of love for the neighbour are twin safeguards against the fury by which power begins to devour itself. In the power of weakness, submission becomes the moment – not of obedient surrender – but of obedient waiting.[11]

Nevertheless, some confrontation is inevitable, because submission to authorities is bound by love's universal demand not to wrong one's neighbour (Rom. 13:7–10). But love can be fulfilled only when anxiety over the decision whether or not to revolt has been removed.

In the confrontation between Jesus and Pilate the issue was: on what authority is power power? The state always validates power in such a way as to justify itself in its use. However, power is not a self-authenticating, autonomous principle. Pilate represents the momentary exercise of power, but Jesus represents its ultimate reality, because he knows its true origin and foundation. Pilate is puzzled that power, if it commands authority, should also require truth. However, in the face of Jesus' silence, Pilate's worldly realism is exposed as pseudo-realism. For when power is divorced from truth its exercise is doomed to self-defeat, because it functions under the spurious authority of self-justification and falsehood.

Jesus, at the point where he is the most defenceless, becomes the judge. His silence unmasks the self-deception of power. He is the harbinger of a revolutionary presence because he stands for the supremacy of truth over power and thus unmasks all hypocrisy (that most deadly of all revolutionary crimes). In the midst of the exercise of power politics, he demonstrates authentic freedom by refusing to evade his responsibility. To Pilate's will-to-power, he opposes a will-to-death.

The revolutionary unhappily shares Pilate's attitude to power, therefore he hurries past the moment of freedom because he fails to discern the patience for freedom required by the fury of his own impatience.[12] . . . When truth confronts the power to crucify with the power to silence it signals to all the world a revolutionary life-style that only silence can express.[13]

[11] *Ibid.*, p. 47.   [12] *Ibid.*, p. 63.   [13] *Ibid.*, p. 66.

If revolutions are to be delivered from the futility of the power they engender in order to achieve their promises, they need to experience a transvaluation of power in a politics of transfiguration.

It is in the transfiguration of Jesus (Mt. 17:1–8) that a truly revolutionary transformation of power is displayed. Jesus by consciously dissociating himself from the passions and practices of the Zealot party shows that he rejects the current interpretation of political messiahship. The difference between their respective views of power is the difference between

> the seizure of power by force in order to establish a new order and the unyielding pressure upon established power, already under judgment for its default of order, in response to the power already ordering all things in a new and humanizing way.[14]

Lehmann finishes his lengthy theological interpretation of revolution by explaining, in the light of Jesus' revolutionary life-style, how he understands the transfiguration of revolution. We can include here only a few of his basic ideas.

> Biblical politics identify transfiguration as the happening according to which the providential-eschatological pressure of reality upon human affairs gives political shape to a divinely appointed new, freeing and fulfilling human order.[15]

Revolutions are signs of transfiguration only when they herald an overdue revision of all political priorities. They show themselves to be authentic or spurious according to how they use power as a policy.

Power can be transfigured only by the liberating story of Jesus, for he has shown that in any test of strength, humility is the strongest kind of power. This 'humiliation in its social and political aspect is supplication'.[16]

A revolutionary movement exhibits its transfiguration in the moment

---

[14] *Ibid.*, p. 91.   [15] *Ibid.*, p. 271.

[16] Here Lehmann quotes from an unpublished doctoral dissertation of Paul R. Valliere, *M.M. Tareev. A Study in Russian Ethics and Mysticism*, *cf.* p. 348, n. 87.

beyond iconoclasm and idolatry towards the regenerative vocation of supplication – *the revolutionaries are the suppliants of history.*

It is at this point that revolutionary and biblical politics converge, making possible (there is no other way) 'a new and fulfilling order in the world.'[17]

Though Lehmann has supplied a good deal of very interesting reflection on past and present revolutionary movements, and has boldly undertaken the hazardous but necessary task of relating the biblical message about Jesus Christ to situations of revolution, he has also given a classic exposition of *theoretical* answers to real-life situations. Lehmann is able to show how the Christian faith, *in abstract*, might be able to help revolutionary strategists and activists overcome the betrayal of their own ideals. He gives us no hint, however, how this might be achieved from within the complexity and ambiguities of change which follow an actual revolution. Could it be that he has fallen into the trap, which intellectuals find particularly difficult to spot, of assuming that the mental acceptance of propositions leads somehow to a change of direction?

The problem with revolutions is that so often they are made by people who are seduced by the logic, beauty and generosity of their own ideas. Every person, but perhaps particularly the highly educated, has a great capacity to be deceived by his own theoretical grasp of reality. When, in addition, he risks a good deal to promote political and social upheaval, the scene is set for an intolerant indisposition to accept any opinion but his own. Only the practical failure to achieve revolution is likely to cause him to reconsider his ideals and the means of implementing them.

Daniel Berrigan

In comparison with the other people we have been studying Berrigan is unique in a number of ways. Firstly, he has not written systematically about Christian involvement in revolution; his thoughts on the subject, which are not lacking in coherence, have been expressed in articles, meditations, letters and recorded discussions, not in closely reasoned and well-documented books. Secondly (and this

---

[17] Lehmann, *op. cit.*, pp. 285–287.

helps to explain the first), he has been what one might loosely call an 'activist'. A good deal of his writing was put together either while he was 'underground' (a 'fugitive from injustice' escaping capture by the FBI) from April to August 1970, or while he was in Danbury Prison, Connecticut, from August 1970 to February 1972. Thus one might justly say that his theological thought has followed the method advocated by Gutiérrez, namely reflection on action in the light of God's Word. Thirdly, he is irrevocably and totally committed to non-violent action as the only means of changing the norms and values of society in a truly revolutionary way. In a letter to the Weathermen he makes this point in a crystal-clear fashion:

> No principle is worth the sacrifice of a single human being . . . I am in the underground because I want none of this inhumanity, whatever name it goes by, by whatever rhetoric it justifies itself . . . I would as soon be under the heel of former masters as under the heel of new ones . . . A revolution is interesting insofar as it avoids like the plague the plague it promised to heal. Ultimately, if we want to define the plague as death, and I think that's a good definition, the healing will neither put people to death nor fill the prisons nor inhibit freedoms nor brainwash nor torture its enemies . . . nor exploit anyone . . . It will have a certain respect for the power of truth, which created the revolution in the first place.[18]

All of our other authors have assumed that 'revolutionary' violence may be employed on certain specific occasions as long as the end in view is a new kind of society.

In May 1968 Daniel Berrigan and eight colleagues began a serious process of civil disobedience by burning draft papers with home-made napalm in a car park in Cattonsville. Their action was intended to be a symbolic act of protest against what they conceived to be the blasphemy of American intervention in the Vietnam civil war. Their motives were Christian:

> Our Gospel led us to the heart of life, we were called upon to stand at the side of the poor, the victimized and the excluded . . . We are pea-

[18] D. Berrigan, *America is Hard to Find* (London, 1973), pp. 95–96.

94

cemakers, the methods of the war are not our methods; its justification is worlds apart from our gospel.[19]

For them the war reflected 'a public philosophy of nihilism and assassination.' The Christian was duty bound to live in constant rebellion against this philosophy on behalf of the victims of 'the absurd and bestiality.'[20]

Their resistance to 'unjust' laws, however, went much deeper than a symbolic demonstration against what they called the immorality of certain property arrangements[21] (*i.e.* the unassailable right of government to dispose of the life of its citizens in the war-game); its intention was to call attention to the perennial American reality of organized violence and greed.[22] It was a frontal attack against the ideology of the 'American dream': those wholly ambiguous values of freedom and plenty which undergird the uninhibited right to consume.[23]

In other words, the war resisters were protesting both against the real causes of American involvement in Vietnam and also against the malaise of a society so effectively able to pacify any potential dissent from the aims of the 'good life'. Berrigan has much to say about the reality of the unconscious forces which drive American society on without there being any serious and lasting attempt to question its direction and methods. America is built on the ideology of success. A feeling is abroad that all problems in the 'great society' can be solved rapidly and efficiently by recourse to the stunning achievements of science, technology and economic management:[24]

> One of the mysterious aspects of the American experience is that we're probably the first people in history who have given over our hopes of immortality to the machine . . . The idea that if your machine is powerful enough and lethal enough, it will destroy enough of the 'enemies of

[19] D. Berrigan, *Lights on in the House of the Dead: a Prison Diary* (New York, 1974).

[20] D. Berrigan, *No Bars to Manhood* (New York, 1970). I quote from the Spanish edition, *Conciencia, ley y disobediencia civil* (Salamanca, 1974) p. 185.

[21] *Lights on in the House of the Dead*, p. 119.

[22] D. Berrigan, *Cf. Absurd Convictions, Modest Hopes: Conversations after Prison with Lee Lockwood* (New York, 1973), p. 184.

[23] *America is Hard to Find*, p. 55; *Absurd Convictions*, p. 26.

[24] *Absurd Convictions*, p. 10.

immortality' to render you immortal. To me this is an undercurrent of the war itself.[25]

The war is the result of a feeling that other values and experiences may well threaten this hope of immortality. When allied to technology war becomes a totally absorbing and totally destructive pursuit. The people's energies must be directed to achieving a wholly successful outcome. That is why Berrigan refers to war as blasphemy and idolatry:

> Violence speaks with the voice of God, with the voice of justice, with the voice of intellectual enlightenment. In such a way, since war by its nature is total today, every structure must be totalized into the main enterprise. So the courts become another instrument of the war itself.[26]

But the state has already become an idol because it 'declares itself good and virtuous in principle and declares others (minorities within the nation and various countries on several continents) to be the enemy.'[27]

Berrigan conceives revolution to be the active involvement of minority groups in society promoting a wholly different view of goodness and virtue. He bases his case on the revolutionary quality of Jesus Christ and the early Christians.

Berrigan sees the modern state as possessing excessive and godlike powers. He therefore interprets Christ principally against the background of resistance to the pretensions of Caesar. Christ followed the path of the prophetic resister: one who categorically opposes all powers which lay claim to unassailable divine authority.[28] The pretensions of Caesar were, and always have been, based on the right of exercising self-vindicating violence in order to maintain the system intact. Christ's revolution consisted in adopting a different life-style. He deliberately chose to put himself on the side of powerlessness, on the side of those who suffer 'authorized' violence. In this way he exposed both the ruthlessness of power and its death-wish:

[25] *Ibid.*, pp. 110–111.   [26] *Ibid.*, p. 204.
[27] D. Berrigan, *The Geography of Faith: Conversations between Daniel Berrigan when Underground and Robert Coles* (Boston, 1971), p. 162.
[28] *Lights on in the House of the Dead*, pp. 164–165.

His nonviolent life excited fury and violence in exact proportion to his restraint, consistency and self-possession.[29]

He gave his life for his brethren, preferring to suffer violence rather than inflict it on others. His final gesture was one of kenosis, offering, the drawing of blood.[30]

Berrigan believes that the violent death of the non-violent Messiah has tremendous implications for Christian activity in the world. It supplies the Christian with a coherent basis for action, namely, that 'in the Christian view of history, the idea that counts is that the freely offered death of one man is worth more in the long run than all of the mechanized powers of hell and earth combined.'[31] This is because God intervened to vindicate Jesus: 'the poor man is the one whose powerlessness calls upon the power of God irresistibly.'[32] This vindication of Jesus in the resurrection is the beginning of a new humanity, for 'Jesus is the authentic hinge upon which time turns.'[33]

The first generation of Christian communities . . . had seen a new man appear, unpromising though his origins were . . . At his deepest he is simply not to be studied biologically, and maybe not psychologically either. He is born not of the flesh, nor of the will of man, but is of God.[34]

This new humanity is possible only in the power of the Holy Spirit whose presence is

to be measured by the fervour of the rejection on the part of Christians of the old forms of power, the old carnal and military and subversive forms that had ruled for so long, and which Christ had broken through on his death.[35]

The power of authentic revolution is the new birth and its symbol is baptism, which 'was originally conceived to mark the adult's

---

[29] *Ibid.*, p. 47.   [30] *Ibid.*, p. 166.   [31] *Absurd Convictions*, p. 112.
[32] *Ibid.*, p. 112.   [33] *No Bars to Manhood*, p. 130.
[34] *The Geography of Faith*, p. 171.   [35] *Ibid.*, p. 171.

passage from one world of values to a community of radically different values.' For the early church baptism was not an exquisite, religious *rite de passage*, but a subversive moral and political choice:

> it was not an abstract question of worshipping the true God or Caesar as god, because Caesar's demands for adulation were expressed very concretely: membership in the armed forces, participation in wars of conquest . . . One who entered the Christian community . . . did so as an act of faith – and with the sure knowledge that he faced trial and death as a traitor who refused to cooperate with government. Those adults had entered with very open eyes upon a way that was very different from the way of paganism, a way they considered not only superior but for which they were willing . . . to sacrifice their human bodies. It was a truly astonishing kind of decision.[36]

Berrigan is, *par excellence*, a protestant, a resister of the blatant manifestations of unregenerate political life: a resistance which confronts the fundamental values upon which this life is built, violence and material greed. He believes that both effective resistance and the promotion of a new order can be accomplished only by joining Christ's 'way', symbolized in the reality of baptism: death to the old values and reception of Christ's power to live out concretely the values of the new man.

> To be a disciple implies one is poor and helpless before the world (and the Church). Practically speaking such a one is forbidden to be a soldier or a rich man . . . His calling is dramatized by the nakedness with which he enters the baptismal waters, and in the laying down of his sword.[37]

---

[36] *Ibid.*, p. 154.
[37] *Lights on in the House of the Dead*, p. 50.

Chapter Seven

Black North America and Black South Africa:
scraps from the rich man's table

North American Black Theology

Because white theologians are well fed and speak for a people who control the means of production, the problem of hunger is not a theological issue for them. That is why they spend more time debating the relationship between the Jesus of history and the Christ of faith than probing the depths of Jesus' command to feed the poor. Human beings were not created to work in somebody else's fields, to pick someone else's cotton, and to live in ghettos among rats and filth.
James Cone, *God of the Oppressed* (1975).

Although the concept of Black Theology did not originate with Cone, he has become one of its leading exponents and champions. In a short time he has written four major books[1] and many articles. Though not all black people would necessarily agree with his view of Black Theology, nevertheless he has become its most readily recognized spokesman.

In this chapter we intend to examine briefly the thought of two of the four books: *A Black Theology of Liberation* and *God of the Oppressed*. They represent his fundamental theological reflection. Though many concepts in the two overlap and interlock, they appear to breathe very different atmospheres. This may be because they were written in different historical contexts (the five years between 1969 and 1974 saw substantial political and religious change in the

[1] J. Cone, *Black Theology and Black Power* (New York, 1969); *A Black Theology of Liberation* (Philadelphia, 1970); *The Spirituals and the Blues* (New York, 1971); *God of the Oppressed* (New York, 1975).

USA) and at different periods of the author's own intellectual pilgrimage.

If we might make a rather ingenuous comparison, the first book is Cone's 'Black Manifesto'. It makes categorical and outrageous statements designed to deflate the sense of superiority shown by white theological thought:

> In order to be Christian theology, white theology must cease being *white* theology and become Black Theology by denying whiteness as a proper form of human existence and affirming blackness as God's intention for humanity.[2]

The second book shows Cone in a more reflective mood, aware of the genuine objections to some of his earlier propositions. In terms of the comparison, it corresponds to Marx's *Outline of a Political Economy* (1858). Using the same analogy we judge that Cone has still to write a mammoth synthesis like that of *Das Kapital*.

The distinction does not imply fundamental differences of perspective. For example, the theological methodology is the same in both cases. We shall begin our analysis there, move on to look at a few of the main themes, and finish by discussing the importance of the different emphases.

Cone's strong criticism of white theology can best be understood by looking first at the background out of which he speaks, secondly at the sources of this theology, and thirdly at its stated purpose.

The background

Black Theology is an attempt to respond to black consciousness from a Christian perspective. Black consciousness was the result of the new sense of dignity, identity and peoplehood which accompanied the civil rights movement from the mid-1950s onwards and came to the fore in the mid-1960s. It signifies a historical reappraisal of the meaning of black existence in North America since the abject slavery of colonial days. This existence began when black people were legally defined as non-humans. Their position and identity were defined for them by their slave-masters. It was they who

---

[2] *A Black Theology of Liberation*, pp. 32–33.

decided that slavery was both their natural lot and the best thing for society.[3]

Even after emancipation (bitterly and violently contested), black people fared little better. They were freed from formal slavery, but were not allowed to become equal under the law. From the Civil War onwards, their history has been one of racial discrimination, ostracism and exploitation. As a result they have experienced much suffering.

Perhaps the most important characteristic of black consciousness is the belief that integration into the predominantly white community, the implicit aim of the civil rights campaign, is not in the blacks' best interests. Integration means accepting the white interpretation of life's meaning and losing black identity. Black Power organizations such as the Black Panther Party and the Black Muslims have put forward the rejection of integration as the highest goal for the future of the black community.

Many people have seen this rejection as of positive value for North American society as a whole. It powerfully and radically called into question those value systems which had made American involvement in the Vietnam War inevitable and caused the younger generation to seek an alternative society through violence or through the new 'drug philosophy'.

But when black people rejected integration they did not simply repudiate predominantly white values. They recaptured a separate cultural identity through emphasis on links with their African past, and also (importantly for theology) by re-evaluating the role of suffering in the life of a people. The two strands came together in negro folk religion which, mainly in the form of music and verse largely derived from the traditional rhythms of Black Africa, expressed both the meaning of suffering and the hope of liberation.

The sources

The point of departure for Black Theology is unquestionably the personal experience of having a black skin in a society characterized by overt or covert racism.[4] The rediscovery of positive values in

---

[3] *Ibid.*, p. 38. Cone is quick to point out that otherwise enlightened men, like Jefferson, were slave-owners.   [4] *God of the Oppressed*, pp. vi, 16.

black history and black culture,[5] as these have moulded a distinctive black community, is part of a global response to this racism. Basic to this process has been black religion:

> In order for the theologian to recognize the particularity of black religion, he must imagine his way into the environment and ethos of black slaves . . . enduring the stress of human servitude, while still affirming their humanity.[6]

Black Theology, then, depends upon the development of black religion, a development quite different from that of white religion. Black religion has not usually been expressed in theoretical and conceptual terms. It has not produced creeds, confessions of faith or dogmatic systems, partly because no black person would have had the time or inclination to write on that level. Rather, it has produced and been sustained by a tradition of songs, stories, sermons and prayers. This is the rich matrix out of which theological thinking for black people must continue to arise:

> Our theology must emerge consciously from an investigation of the sociological experience of black people, as that experience is reflected in *black* stories of God's dealing with black people in the struggle of freedom.[7]

The purpose

Cone expresses this in a multiplicity of ways. They all find their focal point in elucidating and strengthening the struggle of blacks to liberate themselves from the norms of white existence in order to find their true humanity as created black in God's image:

> The task of Black Theology then is to analyse the nature of the gospel of Jesus Christ in the light of oppressed black people so they will see the gospel as inseparable from their humiliated condition, bestowing on them the necessary power to break the chains of oppression.[8]

Black Theology is designed to show that the anxiety for liberation

---

[5] *A Black Theology of Liberation*, pp. 54–63. [6] *God of the Oppressed*, pp. 10–11.
[7] *Ibid.*, p. 16. [8] *A Black Theology of Liberation*, op. cit., p. 23.

expressed in the sources of black religion coincides with the biblical message of God's liberating purpose. In the particular context of black oppression in the USA it also has the task of demonstrating that it is the only possible Christian theology: 'There can be no theology of the gospel which does not arise from an oppressed community.'[9]

This task will bring it into open confrontation with white theology, which is ideologically incapable of realizing that its dependence upon the cultural norms of an expanding, technological free-enterprise society has unconsciously shaped both its content and method:

> Even today, white 'Christians' see little contradiction between wealth and the Christian gospel;[10] white theologians and ethicists simply ignore black people by suggesting that the problem of racism and oppression is only one social expression of a larger ethical concern.[11]

The methodology

Because of its severe criticisms of traditional white theology,[12] it comes as no surprise that Black Theology consciously adopts a different frame of reference: 'It differs in perspective, content and style from the Western theological tradition transmitted from Augustine to Barth.'[13] So Black Theology, because it springs from an environment whose impact is emotional, challenges all theological discourse which has conceptual thought as the essential groundwork of its method. And, because it is also a ghetto theology – one that springs exclusively from the fact that blackness signifies oppression – it challenges white theology's claim to universal validity. If theology is to take seriously God's way of acting in real history, it must take a stand with the poor and against the rich.[14]

Theology's function is to relate the changeless gospel to changing situations, being careful not to confuse the two. That is why the white condition must not be allowed to determine the meaning of

---

[9] *Ibid.*, p. 23.　　[10] *Ibid.*, p. 208.　　[11] *God of the Oppressed*, p. 201.

[12] Cone allows a very few exceptions. He mentions Herzog, *Liberation Theology: Liberation in the Light of the Fourth Gospel* (New York, 1972). Although he does not refer to Latin American Liberation Theology, perhaps he would also allow that this is an exception. The majority of its exponents certainly have a lighter shade of skin.

[13] *God of the Oppressed*, p. 3.　　[14] *Ibid.*, p. 65.

Christ, whose existence, being wholly bound up with the oppressed of the land,[15] can be properly understood only from a position of oppression.

There can be no universalism which is not particular. If white theology maintains that the gospel is equally for all, it will continue to talk in theological abstractions. However, Black Theology, believing that God's revelation in Christ is the only legitimate hermeneutical principle for exegesis, maintains that as the coloured people of America are God's elected poor, the test of a valid *Christian* theology is its involvement in their struggle for freedom.[16] Authentic theology, being inescapably emotional and of a ghetto nature, is 'the Church's reflection upon the meaning of its faith-claim that God's revelation is identical with the historical freedom of the weak and the helpless.'[17]

The main themes

Cone applies his understanding of the theological task more or less consistently to the whole range of subjects which are generally included in any systematic study of theology: God, Christ, man, truth, faith, the future, *etc*. As we should expect, his conclusions usually differ from those of the majority of traditional textbooks. Rather than attempt to summarize all the main strands of his thought, and fail to do them justice, we shall briefly discuss two of the themes to which he gives special attention: the meaning of suffering and the meaning of Christian ethics.

Suffering is basically a problem because it seems not to have any meaning. If God liberates the oppressed from human captivity, why does their suffering continue, and why do black people still live in such wretched conditions? Either God's perfect goodness or his unlimited power seems to be called into question.

The various biblical approaches to the problem of evil are interested not so much in the metaphysical question of its origin as in the practical question of how God intends to solve it. In the struggle for freedom against the forces of oppression, suffering is inevitable.

[15] *A Black Theology of Liberation*, pp. 201–202.

[16] *God of the Oppressed*, pp. 81–82, 135–136. Cone discusses this point at greater length in an article deliberately designed to answer some of his critics, 'Black Theology and Ideology: a Response to my Respondents', *USQR*, 31, 1, Fall, 1975.

[17] *God of the Oppressed*, p. 196.

However, God's inauguration of the divine Kingdom implies his willingness to be involved in *this* suffering. Freedom is already granted as the eschatological gift of Christ's resurrection, but suffering is the effective means for making it real in the concrete events of each succeeding generation.

For the black community suffering is inevitable as soon as black people decide *to be* in spite of the evidence of their *non-being*. Only the involvement of God himself in 'the suffering of his people is sufficient cause for Black People to reject the oppression which produces it. At the same time submittal to suffering as a permanent historical reality, warns Black People against making the white ideological criterion of "winning" the ultimate test of faithfulness to revelation.'[18]

Christian behaviour is not decided by rational principles which all reasonable people accept as good and right, but by God's act of liberation in Jesus Christ. Ethics, therefore, are derived from a theological investigation of the implications of this divine liberation for Christian life in the world. God's will (which comes in the indicative, not in the imperative) is not expressed as a set of rules and principles derived from a philosophical study of the good.

When God delivers the oppressed he demands that they become what he has made them. The criteria of ethical judgment, therefore, can be hammered out only in the community of the victims of oppression – the white man cannot decide what is Christian behaviour. Thus, in the context of slavery and deprivation, neither stealing nor deception, if they were the only way to stay alive, could be called absolute wrongs. Similarly, a literal appeal to Jesus' words and deeds does not make violence wrong, for the real criterion for decision is Jesus' liberating action today. That action can be discovered only by those actively engaged in breaking the bonds of the political and social *status quo*.[19]

The importance of differing emphases
In order to illustrate the differences between Cone's two studies of Black Theology which we mentioned earlier, we shall take his view

---

[18] *Ibid.*, pp. 163–193; *A Black Theology of Liberation*, pp. 143–149.
[19] *God of the Oppressed*, pp. 195–225.

of God and his approach to Scripture as a source of Christian theology.

The first book is provocative, angry, designed to shock. There are no apologies, no qualifications and no attempt at dialogue with positions he contemptuously dismisses as ideological. The second is more cautious, more defensive, more careful to meet objections, though still a considerable apologetic for the rightness of black aspirations and the means to achieve them.

In his *Black Theology of Liberation* Cone comes dangerously close to portraying God as a tribal deity, the exclusive property of black-skinned people. He starts out from the totally unbiblical and gratuitous assumption that, because God defends the oppressed, he 'declares his complete identification with their situation disclosing, to them the rightness of their emancipation *on their own terms*'[20] (my italics). This is based on the equally unbiblical idea (also shared by some liberation theologians) that black people 'are elected because they are oppressed'.[21]

In this first book the fact of oppression is made *the* starting place for speaking about God. God's identification with the cause of black people struggling for liberation, even with Black Power,[22] means that he is prepared to sanction 'emancipation . . . from white oppression by whatever means black people deem necessary.'[23]

But this particular exposition of the meaning of God is akin to certain primitive pagan beliefs. The measure of both existence and right and wrong is man himself, who then calls upon the gods to justify his choices and serve his needs. As succinctly summarized in the following quotation, Cone's view is a crude, pragmatic and arrogant domestication of the sovereign Lord of the universe:

> The sole purpose of God in Black Theology is to illuminate the black condition so that black people can see that their liberation is the manifestation of his activity.[24]

Cone has committed two grave errors in his theological reflection: firstly, he identifies evil entirely with what others do to us, so that God's liberating work is directed exclusively to the overthrowing of

---

[20] *A Black Theology of Liberation*, p. 91.   [21] *Ibid.*, p. 108.
[22] *Ibid.*, p. 92.   [23] *Ibid.*, p. 92.   [24] *Ibid.*, pp. 155–156.

white domination and exploitation;[25] secondly, he maintains that, because white theology is all wrong, its opposite must be all right. This kind of belief, however, ends by reducing theology to the manifestation of sectarian impulses.

Happily in *God of the Oppressed* Cone has become aware of the objection that his theological thought hardly differs from that of the conservative and liberal white American theology which he deplores, in the sense that it also is culturally determined and used as a rationalization for whatever the respective community has decided to do on other grounds.

To meet the objections, he attempts to take Scripture more seriously as the starting-point for truly *Christian* reflection:

> The Bible is the witness to God's self-disclosure in Jesus Christ. Thus the black experience requires that Scripture be a source of Black Theology. For it was Scripture that enabled slaves to affirm a view of God that differed radically from that of slave masters.[26]

Replying later to the question, 'Who is Jesus Christ for us today?' Cone states emphatically that

> There is no knowledge of Jesus Christ today that contradicts who he was yesterday, i.e. his historical appearance in first century Palestine. . . . If it can be shown that the New Testament contains no reliable historical information about Jesus of Nazareth or that the kerygma . . . bears no relation to the historical Jesus, then Christian theology is an impossible enterprise.[27]

Here he lays the only possible foundation for a discussion which is able to criticize and correct partisan subjectivisms:

> if there is no real basis for . . . faith in the historical Jesus, then the

---

[25] Consistent with this reductionist view of sin and salvation Cone postulates that black people are not sinners in any radical sense. Their sin consists only in trying to understand the enslaver (pp. 99–101). This weakens their struggle for liberation and therefore is guilt before the community (but not before God) (pp. 186–193). The logical consequence of this view is that black people do not need personal salvation, but only political, social and economic freedom (p. 72, n. 12).

[26] *God of the Oppressed*, p. 31.

[27] *Ibid.*, p. 115; *cf.* also Cone, 'Biblical Revelation and Social Existence', *Int.* 28, 1974, p. 432.

distinction between . . . claims about God are limited to a difference in
. . social contexts.[28]

Thus while agreeing that a hermeneutical approach to the Scriptures is a necessary response to our cultural situation,[29] we can at
the same time indicate why we believe Cone, and other black (or
white) theologians, are being fair (or unfair) to Jesus. In the first
book the door is slammed in our white faces and locked from the
outside.

African Black Theology

When blacks speak of the affirmation of their blackness, this does not
mean a resigned acceptance. It is an affirmation: Black is Beautiful! For
any person to become authentically black . . . is an experience similar to
rebirth, a total conversion, the participation in the creation of a new
humanity.[30]

Black Theology must be the occasion for the white man's severe self-
examination. It is a rejection of the way the whites express the Gospel.
Unless they turn their attention to the oppressed they will never understand the Gospel. Compatior ergo sum (I suffer with others, therefore,
I am).[31]

For the purposes of this study we shall follow those African theologians who make a distinction between African contextual, or
autochthonous theology and Black Theology.[32] Desmond Tutu, for
example says that

[28] *Ibid.*, p. 118.

[29] *Cf.* his valuable discussion of the 'Social Context of Theology', pp. 39–45.

[30] A. Boesak, *Farewell to Innocence: a Social-Ethical Study on Black Theology and Black Power*
(Kampen, 1976: =*Black Theology, Black Power*, Oxford, 1978).

[31] David Bosch, 'Currents and Crosscurrents in South African Black Theology', *Journal of
Religion in Africa*, 6, 1974.

[32] One observer of African theology believes that neither expression of African consciousness
holds out much promise for the future. He believes that the task of theology in the Africa of
tomorrow is to reflect on the 'questionings of African Socialism'. He sees the transcendental
lyricism of Léopold Senghor's poetry as the kind of matrix out of which theology should be
expressed. At the same time, however, he questions whether the result will be recognizably
theology. *Cf.* Melvyn Matthews, 'Is there an Indigenous Theology in Africa?' *The Kingsman*,
18, 1975–6, pp. 42–50.

108

African Theology happens when African theologians reflect on the experience of a particular African Christian community in relationship to what we would call revelation . . . Black Theology largely arises out of a specific context – the context of Black suffering at the hands of a rampant white racism.[33]

Burgess Carr believes that

Black Theology . . . presents a dual challenge to our Christian style of life. In a profound way, it challenges the preoccupation with African Theology to advance beyond academic phenomenological analysis. . . . It also forces Christians to come to grips with the radical character of the Gospel of Jesus Christ as an ideological framework for their engagement in the struggle for cultural authenticity, human development, justice and reconciliation.[34]

Although, theoretically, Black Theology would be applicable wherever black people on the African continent suffer oppression and exploitation, it has understandably come to the fore in the unique situation of Southern Africa where blacks suffer specifically because of the colour of their skin. At the same time, the cultural and political context of the African continent creates a climate different from that out of which North American Black Theology has grown.

Black Southern Africans would betray their own aspirations as majority peoples if they sought to develop what James Cone calls a 'ghetto theology'.[35] Though currently powerless in terms of political and economic sharing, their overwhelming numerical superiority gives them an important potential power for the future. Perhaps, for this reason, they do not need to assert so stridently the ideology of Black Power. Allan Boesak finds that Cone's (and even more, Albert Cleage's)[36] theology comes close to being a 'religion of Black Power, . . . a theological justification for the political ideological, pseudo-

---

[33] 'African and Black Theologies: what they mean', *AACCB*, Vol. 7, July-August, 1974.
[34] 'The Engagement of Lusaka' in *The Struggle Continues: Lusaka 1974* (Nairobi, 1975), p. 78; also Ananias Mpunzi, 'Black Theology as Liberation Theology' in B. Moore (ed.), *Black Theology: The South African Voice* (London, 1973), p. 131.
[35] J. Cone, *Black Theology and Black Power* (New York, 1969).
[36] A. Cleage, *Cf. Black Christian Nationalism* (New York, 1972).

religious elements of black nationalism.[37]

In a prolonged analysis of the more radical Black Theology of North America, Boesak finds two potential points of disagreement. Firstly, the theological methodology depends too greatly upon certain unverifiable credal affirmations about what God is doing on behalf of the black community. An unconditional loyalty to black people, whatever their circumstances, means that some theologians go far in identifying the aspirations of the oppressed unconditionally with the purpose of God.'[38] Secondly, the overwhelming stress on liberation, although largely justifiable given the particular circumstances of blacks in the USA, may mean that reconciliation is left out of the Christian gospel. Not that Boesak advocates an easy reconciliation which believes that integration is an adequate substitute for just land distribution, equal job opportunities and the ending of economic deprivation.[39] However, he and other South African black theologians recognize that the Christian gospel implies a reconciliation of black and white races in which the former will be liberated from fears and prejudices, and the latter from the ideological justification of unequally distributed privileges.[40] Reconciliation is a long-term goal. More immediately, black people need to be liberated from every sense of cultural and human inferiority.

In Southern Africa, Black Theology has arisen out of the melting-pot of black consciousness. This is a movement among black people which seeks to liberate them from every vestige of a cultural and racial inferiority complex: it is 'an attitude of mind, a way of life whose basic tenet is that the Black must reject all value systems that seek to make him a foreigner in the country of birth and reduce his basic human dignity.'[41]

This 'conscientization' movement is necessary because 'Black people possess a psychological yoke of despondency, helplessness

---

[37] A. Boesak, *Farewell to Innocence*, p. 64. However, see our discussion of Cone's later writings.

[38] *Ibid.*, p. 103.

[39] *Cf.* David Bosch, 'Currents and Crosscurrents in South African Black Theology', p. 15.

[40] *Cf.* for example, Ernest Baartman, 'Was bedeutet die Entwicklung des Schwarzes Bewusstseins für die Kirche?' in T. Sundermeier (ed.), *Christus der Schwarze Befreier* (Erlangen, 1973), quoted by Boesak, *op. cit.*, pp. 64–65.

[41] Ranwedzi Nengwekhulu, 'The Meaning of Black Consciousness in the Struggle for Liberation in South Africa', *Insights: an Occasional Dossier on Liberation Issues* (Nairobi, n.d.).

and dependency which kills initiative, originality and the will of the people.'[42]

Manas Buthelezi describes the context in which black consciousness becomes imperative:

> The fact that Africans, Indians and Coloureds are collectively referred to as 'non-whites' in official terminology suggests that they have the identity of non-persons who exist only as a negative shadow of whites. In a theological sense this means that they are created in the image of the white man and not of God.[43]

If Black Theology is 'a theology of liberation in the situation of blackness',[44] then its first task will be to restore to black people their true human dignity. Such dignity is based on the fact that 'the doctrine of creation entails . . . the Divine affirmation of my uniqueness.'[45] Part of my uniqueness is blackness, and any depreciation of this given reality is an absurd insult to God.

Mpunzi develops this argument from creation by an appeal to the meaning of the Trinity. All people are created in the image of a Triune God where each 'person' is unique and yet one: 'God is not any one of the unique alone. God is the oneness of the community.' Moreover, 'among the three "persons" there is no superiority.' As a theological deduction from this belief,

> man, with his longing for fellowship, will tear down every structure that sets about trying to rule over others; authoritarianism must be destroyed in every one of its manifestations, particularly its racial manifestation.[46]

But the use of theology to furnish a theoretical basis for total human equality and dignity does not go far enough. Even if this helps to achieve human liberation from a false consciousness, the lack of equality of citizenship still remains.

There are three ways by which the ideology and practice of separate development (*apartheid*) might be overthrown. The most obvious, but politically the least viable in South Africa today, is

---

[42] *Ibid.*   [43] 'Apartheid in the Church is damnable heresy', *AACCB*, Vol. 9, 2, p. 37.
[44] A. Boesak, *op. cit.*, p. 113.   [45] A. Mpunzi, *op. cit.*, p. 132.   [46] *Ibid.*, p. 134.

revolutionary violence.[47] The second is the application of total economic sanctions to the country including the withdrawal of all credit
facilities and an investment and trade embargo. The signs are that
such a world-wide strategy is unlikely to be implemented in the near
future and, even if it were, the South African economy could survive
for some time to come. The third is to induce a gradual change of
mentality on the part of whites which would, at the least, bring them
to an open-agenda conference. The achievement of this third possibility could be part of the mission of Black Theology.

If black people need to be liberated from an inferiority complex,
whites have to be liberated from a sense of superiority. The policy
of *apartheid* is undergirded by the belief that the white people possess
a 'divinely given' mission to decide the destiny of the black races. If
this belief is to be sustained it needs to be backed by some kind of
theological rationalization. Certain white theologians[48] have produced this. They argue that God created different races (*i.e.* peoples
with a common descent, cultural heritage and language) in order to
display the wonder of human diversity. Such diversity can develop
its potential freely only if the races are maintained in cultural and
geographical separation (no mixed marriages, no integrated congre-
gations, separate living areas, separate 'homelands'). Separation
rather than integration best expresses the ideal of unity in diversity.

The danger of this evident distortion of the Christian doctrine of
creation lies principally in the fact that it produces 'myths, "principles", grandiloquent ideals and programmes . . . which falsify the
real facts of human existence,'[49] and to counter this danger Black
Theology has a subversive role to play. The title of Boesak's book

[47] This is probably true as long as the white minority can be persuaded that all violence is
Communist-inspired and a direct threat to the values of Western civilization. If there is any
serious crack in the unity of the white population, because, for example, they are persuaded that
the blacks' aspirations for majority rule are legitimate (or, for any other reason), then the strategy
of violence might become effective.

This paragraph on the means for undermining *apartheid* is not meant to give the impression
that the three ways are mutually exclusive. Nor do I want to suggest that they represent a mature
and informed political judgment. My concern is to try to understand the meaning and function
of Black Theology within the political situation as it is today.

[48] *Cf.* A. Boesak, *op.cit.*, pp. 86–92. He refers particularly to the so-called *Landman Report* of
the white Dutch Reformed Church: *Ras, Volk, Nasie en Volk ereverhoudinge in die Lig van die
Skrif* (Pretoria, 1975), and the article by Prof. C. W. H. Boshoff, 'Christian Nationalism' in T.
Sundmeier (ed.), *The Church and Nationalism* (Johannesburg, 1975).

[49] *Ibid.*, p. 92.

suggests that Christian theology in white racist society must undermine the sense of innocence which the whites need if they are to continue to control the majority population.[50]

So effective reconciliation can only be the fruit of a reciprocal process of liberation: liberation from a false consciousness (black is inferior) and from a false ideology (white represents a higher calling).

The deep concern of theology in Southern Africa should be to enable all races to discover the truth that Jesus Christ has overcome every lie which we believe about ourselves, and that he has made possible the creation of one new humanity.

---

[50] A magnificent example of how biblical theology can be used to subvert the whole apparatus of white 'justice and the rule of law' can be seen in *The Trial of Beyers Naudé: Christian Witness and the Rule of Law* (London, 1975). Beyers Naudé, former Director of the Christian Institute of South Africa, through the constant use of Scripture in his defence shows conclusively the total relevance of the biblical message to contemporary political realities.

Chapter Eight

Latin America:
the rich man's table is the poor man's grave

The Theology of Liberation attempts to elaborate the total content of Christianity starting from the demands of social liberation, which anticipates and mediates final liberation in the Kingdom.
Leonardo Boff, *Teología desde el cautiverio* (1976).

The sense of guilt and of mission, which, as we noted earlier, have been two factors in the rise of most revolutionary theologies, occupy a particularly crucial place in the birth and evolution of Liberation Theology.

As members of the Roman Catholic Church in Latin America,[1] acutely sensitive to the enormous inequalities existing between the privileged few and the disinherited masses, certain theological thinkers have become aware, as never before, of their own church's negative reaction to any kind of fundamental change. To explain why the church has rarely, if ever, broken with its traditional commitment to oligarchic political systems,[2] they have developed sophisticated theological and sociological tools of investigation. Liberation theology, then, was born as a movement of protest within the Latin American Roman Catholic Church.

At the same time its unshakable belief in the need for deep changes in the macro-structures of society has been strengthened by the two most radical social documents which the Roman Catholic Church

---

[1] The Theology of Liberation, with a few notable exceptions, has made little impact on Latin American Protestantism. It is interesting to note, therefore, that Juan Luis Segundo does not think that the underlying theological principles, as he understands them, are ultimately compatible with authentic Protestant tradition, cf. *The Liberation of Theology* (New York, 1976), chapter 5, section 3. Some of the reasons are given in our evaluation at the end of this present chapter.

[2] For example, J. L. Segundo, *Acción pastoral latinoamericano: sus motivos ocultos* (Buenos Aires, 1972); E. D. Dussel, *Historia de la Iglesia en América Latina* (Barcelona, 1972).

114

has ever published, *Populorum Progressio* (1967) and the *Medellin Documents of the Latin American Episcopal Conference* (CELAM, 1968). These documents became powerful tactical weapons in the struggle to convince reactionary elements in the church that official teaching on social issues no longer supported their opinions.

Nevertheless, in spite of official changes in Roman Catholic social thinking, certain priests and laymen, personally involved in situations of intractable poverty, began to realize that the official documents did not provide them with a sufficiently thorough analysis of, or response to, the particular problems they were encountering.

Their 'discovery' of the inadequacy of the church's social documents was largely the result of two new factors in their thinking. Firstly, they accepted the current explanation of the causes of underdevelopment being put forward by a new generation of Latin American economists working with Marxist categories of analysis.[3] These economists maintained that underdevelopment, which was actually becoming more marked relative to the developed nations of the capitalist West, was due to the inherently exploitative nature of world economic relations.[4] At least four factors in these relations were causing the *per capita* income gap between rich and poor nations to increase yearly: the repatriation of dividends on capital investments; high interest on loans from the IMF, the World Bank, governments and business consortiums; tariff protection against imports (especially by the EEC); and the wildly fluctuating prices of raw materials. The classical trade theory of potential comparative advantage had to be replaced by a new theory which adequately explained the unilateral advantage of some nations over others. In this way the economic theory of 'dependence' was born. Secondly, they believed that, in the light of increasing poverty and economic exploitation, Christian faith needed to adopt a particular ideological framework to give fresh impetus to its commitment.

Liberation Theology was born, then, as a protest against both the prevailing social and political conditions of Latin America and the easily identifiable structures of class privilege and oppression which

[3] As, for example Darcy Ribeiro, *Las Américas y la civilización* (Buenos Aires, 1972); Gunder Frank, Celso Furtado, Theotonio dos Santos in H. Bernstein (ed.) *Underdevelopment and Development: The Third World Today* (Harmondsworth, 1973).

[4] In the case of Latin America particularly those embodied in the 'Alliance for Progress', launched by John F. Kennedy.

115

caused and maintained them.

Finally, it arose as a sharp protest against the kind of theology being taught and studied in the academic centres of Western Europe and North America.[5]

In order to understand more clearly the underlying motives, methodology and guiding principles of Liberation Theology, we shall analyse more fully, and in reverse order, the reasons for its appearance in Latin America.

The protest against theology

As a fresh attempt to grapple with the theological issues raised by the pressing needs of contemporary Latin America, it has challenged the whole style and purpose of modern theological study.[6] The main aspects of its criticism (which has not spared even the European theologians of revolution) can be summed up in three main points:

First, theology has traditionally been carried out from the perspective of philosophical idealism. This means, in practice, that in discovering the meaning of obedience to God's revelation, theoretical thought is always given precedence over concrete involvement in the world. Behind this stance lie the following premises:

(a) It is possible to carry out intellectual, theological study on a neutral, scientific basis, independent of any particular, personal, ecclesiastical, cultural or ideological conditionings.

(b) Christian personal and social ethics must begin from a theological analysis of a situation which is based solely on Christian sources.

(c) In order to apply the principles of Christian faith to concrete events, bridging the gap between past event and present reality, theology is not obliged to choose any particular socio-political tool of analysis.

Second, theological study easily becomes divorced from the church's obligation to fulfil Christ's mission in the world. In many

---

[5] Cf. the argument of José Miguez in *Revolutionary Theology Comes of Age* (London, 1975), chapter 5: 'Hermeneutics, Truth and Praxis'; J. L. Segundo, *De la sociedad a la teología* (Buenos Aires, 1970), Introducción: una iglesia sin teología.'

[6] The theologians of liberation are not so naïve as to lump all theologies together in the same pot. They allow exceptions to the general methodology they criticize (which, however, also prove the rule). But these exceptions also all spring from a real and costly involvement alongside oppressed groups.

cases it has become an isolated academic discipline, which no longer responds either to the meaning of revelation or to the challenge of human struggles for genuine freedom, but only to certain internal, self-justifying criteria of intellectual excellence. In this sense it is a closed, self-perpetuating academic pursuit, lacking any relevant message for a real world full of conflicts, injustices, prejudices and the abuse of power. If it does concern itself with certain human issues, it is usually to offer advice or make moral pronouncements, often of a condemnatory nature. It is not committed in practice to changing society. It is a theology *about* revolution, rather than a theology *for* revolution. It engages in dialogue *with* Marxists, rather than in programmes of change *alongside* them.

Third, therefore, contemporary Western theology is a largely passive and unconscious instrument of a conservative political and economic system. It can be relied upon to undermine any attempts to interpret God's revelation as demanding a biased commitment to the poor and oppressed. Far from being a neutral discipline of objective historical and linguistic research, contemporary theology, by failing to engage with the most pressing ethical problems of the age, demonstrates itself to be an ally of all forces opposed to change.

The alliance with Marxism

Miguez has explained with great care how Liberation Theology views Marxism.[7] Its initial interest is not in Marxism as a self-contained philosophical system with which, as with any other philosophy, an educated Christian ought to debate. Rather it is a revolutionary theory in the service of action which seeks to change situations and systems of exploitation. Eventually debate with Marxism will be unavoidable because it has evolved, as any consistent humanism must, into a closed, dogmatic, total philosophy of life, antagonistic to the Christian world-view.[8] But this debate is meaningful only within a common commitment to build a different kind of social order.

Marxism has left its mark on the Theology of Liberation in a

[7] *Cf.* J. Miguez, *Christians and Marxists: the Mutual Challenge to Revolution* (London, 1976).

[8] Though their assessment of Marxism might not be as critical as mine, *cf.* the criticisms made by Miranda, *Marx and the Bible: a Critique of the Philosophy of Oppression* (New York, 1974), p. 278ff.; J. Miguez, *Christians and Marxists*, pp. 128ff.; 72ff., 97ff.

variety of ways. It has shown that no theoretical thought is neutral, but is harnessed either for or against revolutionary change. Theology is no exception. It should be used, therefore, as an agent of conflict, making people aware of the real causes of oppression and how the church has tacitly defended the mechanisms which maintain the *status quo*. It has also emphasized the fact that true knowledge of any situation is available only to those committed to change it. This epistemological principle, sometimes called 'action-reflection', means that truth is grasped in experience only as the subject of liberating action. On this basis, authentic theological thought cannot exist for itself but only as a means for promoting movements of liberation. Marxism has shown that only by adopting a particular tool of socio-political analysis can the underlying realities of human relations in the modern world be properly understood. This means that theology can read the meaning of God's actions in present world history only by adopting a particular ideological slant. Finally, it shows how theology has been involved in suppressing knowledge of the real causes of human alienation.

The deliberate use of ideology as a part of theology's task and the church's mission is the most characteristic feature of Liberation Theology. In some ways, left-wing Christian thinkers in Latin America are concerned not so much to produce a new theological synthesis or system as to revolutionize the way in which theological reflection is carried on. Segundo, commenting on three tendencies which together have threatened to destroy Liberation Theology, harassment within the church, domestication of the language of liberation and an over-simplification of theological questions by its main exponents, concludes that perhaps the time for epistemology has arrived, *i.e.* for analyzing, not so much the content as the method itself of Latin American theology and its relation to liberation.[9] For this reason his work *The Liberation of Theology* will probably prove far more significant in the long run than Gutierrez's epoch-making initial study *A Theology of Liberation*. In this book, Segundo explores thoroughly the meaning of Marxism for theological hermeneutics. His discussion helps to clarify Liberation Theology's claim to be a new way of doing theology.

[9] *The Liberation of Theology*, p. 9.

His first premise is that any interpretation of Christian sources, particularly of the Bible, which seeks to be relevant to the church's contemporary mission, must take place from within a hermeneutical circle. This circle has two basic elements: 'our questions and suspicions regarding reality, and a new interpretation of the Bible.'[10]

The interpreter completes the circle by passing through four different stages:

(i) the way we approach reality provokes an ideological suspicion;

(ii) the ideological suspicion is applied to the whole ideological superstructure in general and to theology in particular;

(iii) a new way of experiencing theological reality provokes an exegetical ideological suspicion, *i.e.* the suspicion that current biblical interpretation does not take into account important facts;

(iv) finally, we arrive at our new hermeneutic, *i.e.* the new way of interpreting the source of our faith, the Scriptures, with the new elements at our disposal.[11]

Liberation Theology stands or falls by the legitimacy of approaching biblical interpretation in this way.

Next, we need to see how Marx availed himself of this circle in his classical and fundamental criticism of religion. The first stage is marked by the option between interpreting and changing the world; the second by the discovery of historical materialism as a theory which enables us to discover the true reality of the world, while seeking to change it. This theory teaches that existing beliefs in religion, philosophy, politics and so on, are largely determined by the kind of economic system which the dominant class operates. In the third stage, Marx concludes that religion is wholly at the service of the dominant classes, keeping the oppressed classes ignorant of their true situation and giving them a false consolation for their present sufferings.

For historical, and possibly other reasons, Marx never reached the final stage of the circle. He never suspected that Christian theology was not intrinsically ranged on the side of the exploiting classes, that

[10] *Ibid*, p. 13.

[11] *Ibid.*, p. 14; the numbers are added to the text to help clarify the stages of the hermeneutical process.

its use by them was not due to an inherent defect but to a distortion of its central message. Nor did Marx suspect that Christian faith, through a more faithful interpretation of the Scriptures, could be used as a liberating force in the proletariat's struggle to free itself from the system of wage-slavery.

Liberation Theology's principal task, then, is to supply what is lacking in Marx's truncated use of the hermeneutical circle: correcting his sweeping generalizations in the third stage and following through the creative possibilities of the fourth stage.

Against all the heresies of the church

Liberation Theology has been developing the third stage of the circle by protesting vigorously against both the church's implicit conservative political commitments, in spite of Medellin, and the explicit theological principles which hinder it from seeing its own ideological option for the *status quo*.

The political commitments and theological principles can best be shown by their use in a practical situation. Segundo chooses the example of the Chilean episcopate's attitude to Allende's left-wing government (1970–3).[12]

In questions of social reform the Chilean episcopate was, for a long time, more advanced in its pronouncements than any other sector of the Roman Catholic Church.[13] Early in the 1960s, for example, they denounced on several occasions the endemic injustices of the capitalist system. Ten years later they witnessed a process which, theoretically, could have changed that system by constitutional and peaceful means. This, however, would have required the basic co-operation of the Christian Democrat Party, the holder of the largest number of seats in Parliament. This particular party had, under Frei (1964–70), tried to implement its own 'revolution in liberty' according to a model inspired by the theocentric humanism of Jacques Maritain, based upon the Church's social encyclicals and elaborated by Roman Catholic economists and sociologists.

During Allende's first year of office, the Chilean bishops published

---

[12] *Ibid*, pp. 146–150.
[13] The details can be found in the first chapter of my book, J. A. Kirk, *Liberation Theology*, (London, 1979).

a document called *Gospel, Politics and Socialism*,[14] in which they stated quite categorically that socialism in Chile was no alternative to the then existing capitalist system.

Such a statement might not, at first sight, seem strange, but for the fact that they also stated that the church as such could not decide between the two systems, because the church must be open to the whole Chilean people. In other words, Christian faith should not be forced to serve any particular ideology, as there are many, and are all defective in part. For a Christian a number of different political options may be valid.

Segundo pounces upon this apparently flagrant contradiction and explores some of its implications. If Christian faith unites and ideologies divide, then the former is apparently superior to and more universal than the latter. But if faith is more important than ideologies which seek concrete solutions to profound problems of injustice, it can only mean that the faith spoken of is understood 'as a direct medium of eternal salvation, and ideologies . . . as human options which may threaten this superior value.'

So when the Chilean bishops reject socialism in favour of capitalism, they are obviously not aware that they are using their faith as the basis for choosing a particular theology.

They lack this awareness because for them capitalism is not so much an ideological option as part of the basic order of life. Capitalism, therefore, presents no ideological threat to faith, but the church runs into problems when this basic life-style is challenged by a particular ideology. However, the Chilean bishops' intention is not to repudiate the so-called 'Christians for Socialism',[15] but to maintain that capitalism as a social system is perfectly compatible with Christian faith.

Tragically, Segundo believes, the bishops' anxiety to demonstrate the dangers of socialism to Christian faith – atheism, totalitarianism, *etc.*—have made them forget their former criticism: that the inhuman elements intrinsic to capitalism sprang from a synthesis between faith and ideology which (they now say) is impossible for those who have chosen Jesus Christ.

[14] Santiago, 1971.
[15] *Cf. Los cristianos y el socialismo: primer encuentro latinoamericano* (Buenos Aires, 1973).

We should note that Segundo's criticism of the Chilean bishops is of the same order as Brunner's criticism of Barth's double attitude towards National Socialism and Communism,[16] except that the ideologies involved are different. As Communism, for Barth, did not represent such a temptation to Christians as Nazism, so capitalism, for the bishops, is not such a threat to faith as socialism. Their position, however, is based on a failure to recognize that capitalism is equally as destructive of Christian unity as is socialism.

Segundo draws out the following underlying theological principles from what he feels is this all too typical attitude of the Roman Catholic episcopate:[17]

(a) The Christian faith is primarily a message of the reconciliation of individuals with God.

(b) This reconciliation, which takes place within the church, is the principal work of Christ in the world.

(c) The church's faithfulness to its calling will be measured, therefore, by its efforts to extend the message of reconciliation to as great a number of people as possible.

(d) The fundamental unity of Christians reconciled to God should not be broken by political options which, by their nature, are partial and personal.

(e) All social attempts at changing man's existing situation are destined to ultimate frustration and failure, for they presuppose only the natural and not the supernatural causes of evil.

(f) The church represents that new order in the world which God alone can effectively accomplish. Every attempt by man to produce something qualitatively different inevitably leads to idolatry and the founding of counterfeit churches.

Needless to say, Segundo rejects these principles, not on the ground that they are theologically unorthodox, for this would involve him in an idealistic approach to the truth of Christianity, but because they have arisen in this form as part of an ideological superstructure of oppression, and are employed to prevent any real change in this structure. They are not so much false ideas as deformed versions of a total truth which is authenticated by its power to

[16] Cf. ibid, p. 45.

[17] He also believes that the same principles are largely shared by the Latin American evangelical churches, cf. ibid, pp. 151–157.

liberate man from every enslavement and alienation.

In his critique of particular actions and theological principles, Segundo has prepared the way to pass from the third to the fourth stage of the hermeneutical circle. In this final stage he intends to show concretely how the biblical text should be interpreted so that it can no longer be used to neutralize ideologies of change and also how it contributes its own dimension to this change.

Liberating the Bible

None of the theologians of liberation, except José Miranda,[18] has engaged in detailed exegetical study of the biblical text. Segundo, however, does give us an interesting example of how the hermeneutical circle functions. His argument illuminates the way in which he, and others, view the contemporary, central task of theology.

The subject chosen is the relation between Christianity and violence.[19] Segundo begins his analysis of this problem by posing the hermeneutical question: how should we understand today the concrete content of the mutual love which Jesus commanded?

Two main opinions have been given: firstly, Jesus' actions and teaching specifically depict what kind of love is required; secondly, Jesus does not specify the universal content of mutual love, but allows people to choose according to the different circumstances in which they live. In the second case, certain passages from the Gospels (*e.g.* the parable of the good Samaritan) do not tell us how to love, or even to love everyone equally, but that everyone is potentially our neighbour. The only rule is that love should be as efficient and far-reaching as possible.

The conditions for mutual love are circumscribed by a person's particular physical resources. It is possible to love only a limited number of people, in the sense of giving them time and consideration. The rest we relate to impersonally, usually through a given

---

[18] Cf. *Marx and the Bible* (I have written an extended review article on this book for the journal *Sojourners*, Jan. 1977); also *Being and the Messiah* (New York, 1977). I have devoted some twenty pages of my book *Liberation Theology* to an examination of Miranda's exegesis and hermeneutical procedure.

[19] J. L. Segundo, *op. cit.*, pp. 175–205. We are using this example as illustrative material of a particular hermeneutic, not as part of the argument for or against violence (*Cf.* below, Appendix B: 'Violence: Business as Usual?').

society's legal system. When we deal with people impersonally it is because we have chosen to prevent them from becoming our neighbours. If our relationship to the great majority of people is through the law this is only finally possible if the law is upheld, and for this to happen we create coercive structures. In other words, love is a possibility only if we are prepared to use violence or pay others to do so on our behalf. Thus violence can become an instrument of love, in principle quite neutral. Used in this way it is not necessarily the result of selfishness or hate.

The point of this discussion is to demonstrate that, in practice, the question of violence is more subtle and complex than the usual arguments allow. Hermeneutically speaking, Segundo has made what he terms a phenomenological study of violence *before* confronting the biblical text. The next step is to engage in a biblical exegesis of violence.

Segundo insists that because Jesus was truly a man his physical resources were as limited as any other human being's. This meant, for example, that when John the Baptist was imprisoned Jesus was not able to identify himself with John's cause. Segundo thinks that it was this attitude of Jesus, who was supposedly 'the man for others', which caused John to question whether or not he really was the Messiah (Mt. 11:3).

Jesus committed the same kind of violence when he commanded his disciples to extend their mission only to Israel (Mt. 10:5–6) (implying a division between the Jews and the Samaritans and the non-Jews) and when he rebuked the Syrophoenician woman (Mk. 7:27). On the basis of these examples, Segundo concludes that 'without this violence love also dies and human beings float at the mercy of an even greater violence.'[20]

The difference, then, between Jesus' use of violence and its use from motives of selfishness and hate does not lie in the *means* through which it is expressed. Jesus' impersonal, collective and general condemnation of all Pharisees as 'you hypocrites!' (Mt. 15:7) was an example of a common use of violence.

Segundo's first approach to the biblical text, then, shows that Jesus was also subject to physical limitations, and that therefore he too

[20] *Ibid.*, p. 186.

was bound to participate in the violence common to all men. Next he seeks to deal with the problem (for those who believe that physical violence is permitted to Jesus' followers) of the absolute non-violence enjoined by the Sermon on the Mount. Segundo solves this problem for himself by comparing the warnings of Matthew 5:21–22 – 'everyone who is angry with his brother . . . whoever insults his brother . . . and whoever says, 'You fool!' . . . ' – with Jesus' own attitude to the perverse generation who refused to repent (*e.g.* Mk. 3:5; 7:6; 8:38). He concludes that 'what we find in the Bible about violence or non-violence are ideologies', *i.e.* means put at man's disposal to exercise love in the most effective way possible. What is permitted biblically, with regard to means, is what is most convenient in a particular situation (Rom. 14:1–21; 1 Cor. 8:7–13; 10:23–33).

Segundo's final approach to a hermeneutical study of violence in the Bible is general and *a priori*. Continuing to attack all arguments that see in Jesus' own teaching and life an absolute norm for the Christian's attitude towards the use of violence, he delivers what he considers a mortal blow to such an interpretation by declaring that in fact we have no certain access to revelation anyway:

> in other words, to declare that that particular life and teaching contains absolute value appears to presuppose that we can recognize it with absolute certainty. This idea conflicts with the relativity of a thousand historical judgments which are the necessary logical basis for affirming that there has been a real encounter with God in the midst of human history.[21]

Here we leave the exposition of liberation theology as it seeks, in its present phase, to liberate theology from all vestiges of speculation so that it may become an instrument of man's total liberation. In the final section we want to evaluate the goals and achievements of the process, hoping thereby to contribute a different perspective to the debate.

Liberation theology and Protestant misgivings

In stating that a Protestant theologian, in so far as he is faithful to his own heritage, is bound to hold ultimate reservations concerning

[21] *Ibid.*, p. 193.

certain aspects of Liberation Theology, Segundo has discovered an important truth which has not yet been sufficiently elaborated. The main reason for the reservations, he believes, is a different view of the relationship between historical action and the Kingdom of God.[22] Whereas the Reformation doctrine of salvation by faith alone undermines and relativizes all human action, making it less significant than God's action in effecting man's liberation, the Roman Catholic doctrine of merit implies that man's efforts, with the help of God's grace, are effective in the establishing of the Kingdom here and now.

Segundo is partially right. The Reformers' understanding of salvation was founded on their understanding of the nature of man's alienation. Their view of the radical and total nature of sin led them to question very seriously the worth of all man's efforts to change his personal and social situation. As man was wholly corrupted through the fall, his merits were seen as part of this corruption: an attempt to gain righteousness apart from God's free gift of salvation. This was taken simply as further proof of his rebellion.

However, Segundo is only partially right, for the Reformers also elaborated a strong doctrine of 'good works' (calling or vocation). This was seen in the context of the new order which God was creating in response to the unmerited love of Christ in offering himself for the sins of the world. This doctrine of 'good works' is often understood today as 'service', putting oneself unselfishly at the disposal of one's neighbour. Segundo, however, does not consider that this kind of response to the challenge of change today is, strictly speaking, revolutionary.

Segundo also finds difficulty with Protestant theology because it has been unable to break away from its 'idealistic' moorings. He believes that only Roman Catholics have managed to achieve this

---

[22] J. Miguez devotes a whole chapter of his book *Revolutionary Theology* to this very question. Though it is not his intention, he comes very close to a completely monistic view of history. The reason for this, I feel, is his attempt to do justice to one of the main emphases of Liberation Theology. When, however, he is not being defensive, he makes statements which clearly show his acceptance of the eschatological reserve which implies a two-dimensional view of existence. No other representative of Liberation Theology, for example, has adopted an attitude to Marxism as an agent for liberation which would allow him to say the following: 'Nobody (whether Marxist or not) can become a Christian without repentance and conversion. Not a conversion from Marx to the Church, but from sin to Jesus Christ. This movement entails a submission of the totality of life, including one's philosophical understanding or political allegiance, to the grace and judgment of the Lord.' *Christians and Marxists*, p.T126.

fundamental break by making theology 'a critical reflection on Christian praxis in the light of faith'. Theology is a second step which follows 'real charity, action and commitment to the service of men.'[23] However, the situation is not quite so clear cut, and the theologians of liberation may be deluding themselves at this point. For the sake of furthering a dialogue whose object is also the renewal of theology we shall state how we see the issues.

Let us begin by saying that much of Liberation Theology's protest against modern theology is absolutely valid. Since the Enlightenment, theology, like every other discipline, has sought to gain independence from the control of the church in order to pursue its studies according to its own canons and methods.[24] To do this it unhesitatingly accepted the 19th-century emphasis on the inviolability of the scientific method. It isolated itself in the theological faculties of the state universities (especially in Germany) and insulated its work from the daily life and mission of the Christian community.

The reasons for this declaration of independence are complex and cannot be fully investigated here. Undoubtedly, theological thought needed to be relatively free to criticize and change ecclesiastical traditions, dogmas and practices, as well as to engage with other academic disciplines in a general pursuit of truth.

Nevertheless, 19th century theology was blissfully unaware, as were other analogous disciplines, of the very deep ideological and cultural conditionings which animated its work. Critical of the church's conservatism and anti-intellectualism, it was totally uncritical of its own positivist and liberal premises. The situation did not greatly change until the Marxist tradition of ideological suspicion began to influence European and Latin American political theologies.

By isolating itself from the struggles of ordinary Christians to relate their faith to a new, complex and changing society, theology became over-intellectualized and rationalistic. Responding to certain culturally determined academic pressures, theology interpreted the reality of the (Western) world too unilaterally in terms of secularism, and as a result often became an ideological exponent of the growth

---

[23] Gutiérrez, *A Theology of Liberation* (London, 1974), pp. 11–15.
[24] An interesting illustration of this has been the struggle within the Roman Catholic Church, from the beginning of the century until 1943, to allow elements of 'higher' criticism to be officially accepted into Catholic biblical exegesis.

and development of the Western way of life. Theologians' own lack of self-criticism evolved into a lack of criticism of the system which supported their privileges. Modern theology has been unable to concern itself too much with changing the system, for this would imply a radical change in its own situation and self-understanding.

All this has been exposed and challenged, timidly at first by the European theologians of revolution, and then more drastically by the liberation theologians. We hope that this challenge will not be ignored, but reviewed with the seriousness demanded by a theology committed to God's calling.

Nevertheless, although Liberation Theology's critique of contemporary theology is just, it has not yet supplied a wholly viable alternative, because of the quite impossible dichotomy it makes between idealism and materialism, and between theory and practice. In fact no theology is able to reflect upon a pristine practice; all practice is already the result of some kind of ideological and cultural conditioning.

We have said that the most significant aspect of Liberation Theology is its use of Marxism as an ideological tool in liberating theology and, as a consequence, liberating the church to become an instrument for change in society. We have also described how it uses the hermeneutical circle to achieve this end. But how does this methodology avoid being an idealistic approach to reality? One might agree that, as a description of historical causation, the Marxist analysis of the evolution of different economic systems into capitalism has much to commend it. It is difficult to deny that the interpretative tool of 'dependence' most adequately describes the economic situation of the underdeveloped countries in the Third World today. Here we find a useful formula: the reasons for underdevelopment = the recent history of the underdeveloped + an adequate interpretation. However, the model of 'dependence' is not a specifically Marxist one, nor does commitment to some kind of socialist solution to widespread poverty and unjust distribution of wealth necessarily imply a Marxist society. Indeed commitment to Marxism involves a whole set of assumptions, ranging from the class struggle to the withering away of all coercion in a classless society, which have absolutely no basis in empirical fact.

Liberation Theology has confused what is empirically verifiable in the Marxist analysis of economic relations with what, in a fuller Marxist creed, belongs to the superstructure (*i.e.* is conditioned by Marx's and subsequently Lenin's own historical circumstances). Here the exponents of Liberation Theology have proved themselves as susceptible as anyone to accepting theories which have been shown to be incongruous with reality.

Unfortunately, it is often the theory, rather than the tested facts, which are made to orientate the hermeneutical task. Just as Marx's belief in an evolution of capitalism, first into socialism and then into full Communist society through the expropriation of the means of production by the labouring classes, is pure speculation, so also is Liberation Theology's belief in man's ability to change history in the direction of the Kingdom of God.

There is another, more crucial aspect of this relationship between theory and practice. What are the grounds for undertaking the liberation of theology by using the Marxist ideology to complete the hermeneutical circle? The facts of exploitation are eloquent, but they are powerless to provide a motive to struggle against them. It is a fundamental fact of man's ethical experience that both the reasons for liberating man and the methods to be employed have to be justified *a priori*, according to values which are themselves justifiable or not, and open to question or not. Marxism as a so-called scientific analysis of economic realities cannot provide these values, for right and wrong cannot be decided on empirical grounds alone. That is why Marxism has had to become not only an economic theory but a total world-view, able to give a reason for the necessity of revolutionary change and inspire men and women to heroic efforts of self-sacrifice to bring it about.

Acceptance of the need to liberate theology by using the Marxist ideology is decided on the basis of a theoretical, ethical choice, which is made prior to actual involvement in a liberating process – for how does one know that that particular political action is in fact *liberating*? Behind the choice is the whole weight of Christian tradition, as it is in a more veiled form behind Marx's outbursts of righteous indignation. Pure historicism—the mere objective description of the so-called 'iron laws of history'—is totally inadequate to motivate truly revolutionary change or decide the meaning of liberation.

It is understandable that Liberation Theology is hesitant to use categories of revelation in the struggle to put theology at the service of liberation, because of the past and present ideological manipulation of theology (including the categories of revelation). However, in order that the fourth stage of the hermeneutical circle may operate freely and theology become a total liberating tool, revelation is the only possible final ground of appeal. There are two important reasons why this is so. Firstly, Marxism itself is not exempt from its own charge of producing a false consciousness and an illusory hope (it may well prove to be the 20th century's 'opium of the people'), for its belief that a truly equal, free and just society will develop from the ashes of capitalism is a mythological story of recreation in the future. The reasons for historical development are not adequately covered by a dialectical-materialist understanding of history, but only by biblical revelation, which alone unfolds the primary cause of man's alienation. Secondly, Marxism is a very limited tool for the liberation of theology, because although it may ask provocative questions and make true accusations, theological methodology can only be changed from within, *i.e.* as a necessary response to the challenge of its own subject-matter.

Unfortunately, Liberation Theology, with very few exceptions, has not yet taken seriously the power of the unadulterated biblical message to bring to mankind a complete liberation. The inadequate attention given to biblical exegesis as a liberating task means that the fourth stage of the hermeneutical circle is still cut short. The only way, we believe, of reaching a profounder understanding of reality as history plus its interpretation is by applying ourselves to this task.[25]

---

[25] We shall attempt to develop further the reasoning behind our criticism of the main weaknesses of Liberation Theology in chapter 10, 'A Question of Method.'

APPENDIX A

The World Council of Churches:
programme to combat reactionaries?

As to whether we should centre upon individual conversion or upon social change to realise the Kingdom we reply that we must do both.
Report of the International Missionary Council, Tamboram
(1938).

It is more difficult to discover a coherent approach to the question of theology and revolution in a complex body like the WCC, made up of many different interlocking departments, commissions and projects, than in the work of an individual theologian.

We may note two particular difficulties. First, what constitutes an official pronouncement of the WCC and what validity does it have as a statement of opinion? Second, is there a sufficient consensus in WCC circles on the question of revolutionary change to be able to say that one particular position is being held?

Paul Bock, in his valuable book *In Search of a Responsible World Society: the Social Teachings of the World Council of Churches*,[1] has devoted a chapter to 'The Nature and Purpose of World Council Pronouncements'. He notes that the WCC produces two kinds of document, according to the kind of meeting from which it springs. There is the document which speaks unofficially *to* both the churches and the WCC: such would be, for example, the final document of the 1966 Geneva Conference on Church and Society.[2] This kind of document is tentative and exploratory and tends, naturally, to reflect more than one viewpoint. Then there are the documents which speak officially *for* the WCC to the churches. At the risk of over-simplification, we may sub-divide these into three further groups: the reports of official commissions, like Faith and Order; the reports of

[1] Philadelphia, 1974.
[2] *World Conference on Church and Society: Official Report* (Geneva, 1966).

the septennial Assemblies; and the reports adopted by the Central Committee at its annual meeting. Of these, the last has the most right to be considered the official voice of the WCC. Nevertheless, as Bock points out,

> Ecumenical leaders never claimed that their statements are binding on member churches or individuals. . . They are the product of careful deliberation by a council of Christians of different denominations from all over the world. Their findings might be expected to carry considerable informal authority for the Churches. . . The authority of 'their own truth and wisdom'.[3]

On the question of consensus we have to assume what we lack space to prove, namely that there exists a large measure of agreement in those WCC documents which, since the mid-1960s, have addressed themselves to the broad area of social ethics. Circumstantial proof of this can be found in the overwhelming approbation given by the Fifth Assembly (Nairobi, 1975) to the highly controversial Programme to Combat Racism (325 votes to 62).

We mention the mid-1960s because, since that time, a notable shift of emphasis in the WCC's social concern may be detected. Probably the main reason for this has been the changed make-up of the constituent churches. The inclusion, firstly, of the Eastern (and especially Russian) Orthodox Churches in 1961 altered the WCC's previous tendency to view world political reality mainly in the context of the East-West cold war. Secondly, the admission to membership of a growing number of Third World churches changed the areas of concern to a North-South axis.[4]

No conference has caused such a deep and sustained impact upon the WCC as the 1966 Geneva Conference on Church and Society.[5] The purpose of the conference was set out by the Central Committee in 1962:

[3] Bock, *op. cit.*, pp. 22–23.

[4] *Cf.* H. Berkhof, 'Berlin versus Geneva: our Relationship with the Evangelicals', *ER*, 28, 1976, p. 83; Bock, *op. cit.*, pp. 46, 146.

[5] This was followed two years later, in conjunction with the Roman Catholic Church's Pontifical Commission on Justice and Peace, and under the auspices of SODEPAX, by another conference in Beirut, on the same set of issues, *cf.*, *Peace: the Desperate Imperative* (Geneva, 1970). On the important work of SODEPAX, *cf.* Joseph Spae, 'Sodepax: an Ecumenical and Experimental Approach to World Needs,' *ER*, 26, 1974, pp. 88–89.

The time has come to look at the problems of society in the modern world from the perspective of God's call to man and thus to help to develop a body of theological and ethical insights which will assist the Churches in their witness in contemporary history.[6]

Its main significance lies in the fact that it became a definitive point of departure for subsequent reflection. The ripples it set in motion later became gigantic waves that on occasions have threatened to engulf the good ship *Oikoumenē*.

Three particular issues surfaced at that time. Firstly, there was a new awareness that contemporary theological methodology was not geared to a creative interaction with the technical and social sciences. The active participation of many lay people, highly qualified in different social, political and technological fields, highlighted the churches' abysmal lack of experience in the field of interdisciplinary discussion and research. As M. M. Thomas and Paul Albrecht state in their introduction to the documents:

> The cooperation of theologians with laymen was very problematical as so little has been previously made of the lay-understanding of modern society in determining the issues on which theological reflection is needed. . . The search for a new method of theological enquiry and study in relation to Christian social ethics is still in the process of development.[7]

Secondly, the first stirrings of disappointment over the failures of modern technology to solve the outstanding problems of poverty began to be felt. This was coupled with a growing awareness that increasingly sophisticated technology is of mixed benefit to man. On the one hand, the early 1960s saw the decline of 'theological realism' (whose mentor was Reinhold Niebuhr) as a basis for Christian social ethics, and the rise of 'the theology of secularization' inspired particularly by van Leeuwan's massive historical analysis of the rise of secularization.[8] This latter valued the birth of the modern secular and technological revolution in the West very highly. Its underlying philosophical basis is the Christian view of creation which has been capable of overcoming all rival notions of man's relation to nature.

[6] *Church and Society: Official Report*, p. 8
[7] *Ibid*, p. 40.   [8] *Christianity in World History* (London, 1964).

Thomas and Albrecht, in the same introduction, stress the need for a Christian social ethics which assimilates and is more challengingly relevant to the new secular humanism.[9] On the other hand, others began to demonstrate that the complex, autonomous forces of modern technology were becoming increasingly impersonal and dehumanizing.[10]

Thirdly, and most importantly, the Geneva Conference saw that the failure to solve the problem of increasing poverty was due not to technological limitations but to the developed countries' lack of political will to hand back some of their accumulated riches, gained at the expense of former colonized peoples. The significance of accepting this reason for poverty does not lie in its use of revolutionary terminology to express it (for example, the struggle for social and economic justice), nor in its willingness to accept certain aspects of the Marxist critique of contemporary capitalism,[11] but in the radical shift of perspective which is implied. We shall now try, briefly, to assess the meaning of this shift.

Fundamentally, it has involved a new attitude towards history. Instead of accepting unconsciously the prevailing Western semi-deterministic attitude to 'progress', it has advocated a prophetic stance towards historical change. This means that theological premises are being used to construct an ethic of change which denounces the blatantly cynical materialism and selfishness of the ideology of progress. This critique also implies a certain shift of emphasis on the theological front.

Since the first Assembly of the WCC at Amsterdam (1948), the guiding principle for ecumenical social concern has been the idea of 'the responsible society'. As Dr Visser 't Hooft stated at Geneva,

> The Ecumenical movement has through its discussion of social problems and its development of the idea of a Responsible Society, discovered an

---

[9] *Church and Society: Official Report*, p. 12.

[10] *Cf.* The *Report* of the Department of Church and Society to the 23rd meeting of the Central Committee held at Canterbury 1969. The increasing concern has given rise to a series of studies on 'the implications of science-based technological change for the future of man and society.' For example, David Gill, *From Here to Where? Technology, Faith and the Future of Man* (Geneva, 1970), and the research conducted by David Jenkins under the title 'Humanum Studies', *cf.* D. Jenkins, 'Man's Inhumanity to Man: the Direction and Purpose of the Humanum Studies', *ER*, 25, 1973, pp. 5–28.   [11] *Cf.* Bock, *op. cit.*, p. 147.

134

ethical criterion for creative action on the problems of our world. Today it must be renewed and reinterpreted in view of the need for a responsible world community and demands for international economic justice.[12]

The Amsterdam Assembly defined the meaning of the responsible society in the following terms:

> For a society to be responsible under modern conditions it is required that the people have freedom to control, to criticize and to change their governments, that power be made responsible as widely as possible through the whole community.[13]

The definition is in many ways closely tied to the Western democratic ideal. This ideal may be far from realization in the West, where the subtle play of political and economic power tends to reduce popular participation to at best a pious hope, and at worst a dangerous illusion; but at least it has its roots in the biblical view of man. This latter rejects man's easy excuses for his permanent social irresponsibility and the fatalistic attitude towards life from which they are derived. Man is a creature called into being to cooperate with his creator's special purpose for history. He is made responsible for the way he treats his fellow men. So, he is unable to take refuge in the ultimate excuse for not promoting change towards a more human society, namely that he is a slave of the system and captive to its structures.

By the time of the New Delhi Assembly (1961), less insistence was made upon the intrinsic benefits of Western democracy. Former colonies, in their struggle to achieve a mature national consciousness, recognized that different political systems would probably be needed:

> The difficulty of maintaining order, of avoiding civil strife, of establishing governments strong enough to deal with the desperate need for economic development, may call for new forms of political life.[14]

---

[12] *Church and Society: Official Report*, p. 13.
[13] Bock, *op. cit.*, p. 69.
[14] *The New Delhi Report* (London, 1961), p. 100.

The Geneva Conference with an obvious allusion to Western Democracy stated that

> as Christians we must neither sacralize nor depreciate the state: states are human institutions that should exist for the well-being of people. They have no eternal nature or form, but should be adaptable to changing history and changing needs. Our task is to participate in them both appreciatingly and critically.[15]

So the WCC no longer ties its vision of a responsible society to the much publicized advantages of parliamentary rule. Over the years it has become increasingly concerned about the deep ethical and theological problems thrown up by the covert manipulation of power and maintenance of privilege at any cost by those nations which claim to be the misunderstood champions of Western values (Brazil, Chile, the Philippines, South Africa, South Korea, etc.). This shift implies a disenchantment with the sincerity of the Western nations' political intentions and a categorical championing of those who are excluded by these same nations from major decisions regarding their own future.

The highly controversial Programme to Combat Racism (PCR) is a good illustration of this shift and the theological thinking which has accompanied it. The PCR developed out of the Secretariat on Racial and Ethnic Relations, created in 1959 as part of the department on Church and Society. The first step towards the creation of a special fund came in the Central Committee's call to the churches (Enugu, Nigeria, 1965) to contribute to the legal defence of the victims of unjust accusations and discriminatory laws in South Africa and elsewhere.

The victims of racial discrimination are considered in WCC thought to be the most degraded of all the world's exploited.[16] On the very lowest level of such discrimination are the blacks oppressed by white minorities who are prepared to use almost any means to

---

[15] *Church and Society: Official Report*, p. 117.

[16] R. Mehl, for example, in the debate at the 1969 Canterbury meeting of the Central Committee said that racism should not be 'confused with other kinds of injustice or rationalized as a conflict between rich and poor or between social classes. It is not only a matter of flesh and blood, it is a matter of demonic powers.' *Minutes and Report* (Geneva, 1969), p. 36.

keep themselves in power. That is why the PCR has given much (but by no means exclusive) attention to Southern Africa.[17]

The first theological defence of the PCR is the statement made by the Uppsala Assembly (1968) that 'the Word of God testifies that Christ takes the side of the poor and oppressed.'[18] This idea implicitly rejects the old liberal presentation of Jesus as the 'man for others', popularized in John Robinson's celebrated book *Honest to God* (1963).[19] Jesus is not the man for others in a vague, all-inclusive, sentimental fashion, for when 'the others' are the authors of racism, the most oppressive of all human systems, he can only be *for* them by being rigorously *against* them.[20]

The PCR, then, is the response of Christian discipleship to the compassionate ministry of Jesus Christ. Compassion is shown not only by a healing ministry where racial passions already run high, but more particularly by a preventive ministry which seeks to forestall manifestations of racial prejudice and antagonism. This is why the PCR's main aim is to investigate the causes of racism in order to discover ways of preventing it.

The PCR is also the response of a servant Christian community to the question of power, for it is a deliberate gambit by which Christian people risk their reputation, wealth, status and even life itself for the sake of the down-trodden and subjected.[21]

The second theological defence springs from the confession that Jesus Christ has already defeated the powers of this present age. The Uppsala Assembly identified these powers as unjust political and economic structures created by human greed, fear, arrogance and selfishness. The Nairobi Assembly calls them 'destructive forces

[17] A full account of the aims and activities of the PCR is given in Appendix VII of the *Minutes and Report* of the Addis Ababa meeting of the Central Committee (1971) (Geneva, 1971), and Appendix VIII of the Central Committee's Geneva meeting (1973): 'Programme to Combat Racism: a Background Paper.' The criteria on which grants are given to different agents are set out in the *Minutes and Report* of the 29th meeting held at Geneva in 1976.

[18] *The Uppsala Report*, p. 61.

[19] *Cf.*, for example, *Breaking Barriers: Report of the Nairobi Assembly* (London, 1976), p. 130: 'In the person of Jesus Yahweh has put himself decidedly in the place of the poor; he has searched for those who are "nothing" (1 Cor. 1:26–31).'

[20] In a different context from that of the WCC, Jon Sobrino in his book *Christology at the Crossroads: a Latin American Approach* (London 1978) makes the same point, *cf.* pp. xv ff.; 41.

[21] *Cf. Church and society: official report*, p. 209; also *Minutes and Report* of the 24th meeting of the Central Committee, Addis Ababa (Geneva, 1971), p. 55.

at work throughout the human family' which give a taste of 'the principalities and powers'. Later it identifies them more concretely with (among other things) transnational corporations, partly because these achieve a high concentration of economic and technical power in the hands of a few. This power seems to be constantly reinforcing itself and to be completely outside the control of those whom it negatively affects. 'They are a typical example of the way in which capitalist forces . . . join forces to oppress the poor and keep them under domination.'[22] By their massive investments they help to keep the economies of racially segregated societies afloat. The unification of international capitalist exploitation with extreme racist societies is another reason for the extra attention given by the PCR to Southern Africa.[23]

But Christ has conquered these particular powers. The Christian is called to live by the certainty that the coming Kingdom is a more powerful reality than all the forces of destruction, deprivation and death which man manipulates in a vain attempt to control his destiny without his Creator. In this sense, the PCR is a visual testimony to the fact that a Christian has thrown off the grip of blind fate, knowing that mankind need no longer submit itself to the rule of suprapersonal, tyrannical forces:

> Jesus is our liberator inasmuch as . . . he gives us hope, i.e., he affirms the right to life and the triumph of life against cynicism and fatalism of the pure politics of power . . . We are not faithful to Jesus Christ when we submit to the powers that be. . .[24]

This short discussion of the PCR is not intended as a blanket defence of everything it stands for.[25] Rather, its purpose has been

[22] *Breaking Barriers*, pp. 101, 130–131.

[23] At Nairobi it was stated: 'the grip of racism is today as acute as ever, because of the institutional penetration, its reinforcement by military and economic power and because of widespread fear of loss of privilege by the affluent world.' *Ibid*, p. 133.

[24] *Ibid.*

[25] Whereas there is much in the PCR which ought to commend itself to all sensitive Christian consciences, especially money given both to programmes of research into causes of racism and to the defenceless victims of racism in various parts of the world, nevertheless financial donations to guerrilla groups in Southern Africa have stretched Christian credulity.
Perhaps no more need be said here than that it is, at best, extremely ironic that groups which, like the ones mentioned below, have been or are supported by money from Christian sources,

to show the way in which certain theological considerations are made the spring-board for a particular course of action. The same kind of interaction between theory and practice is found in other areas of the WCC's revolutionary social concern, such as the use of modern technology in underdeveloped regions of the world, the concept of a sustainable society, the significance of a simple life-style, human rights and the use and abuse of property.

This interaction is still at a tentative stage, for the WCC in its reports, programmes and projects seems to be seeking a substantial renewal of theological methodology,[26] which would bring theology into a dynamic relation with the real sufferings, struggles and needs of what Philip Potter has referred to as the 'Two-Thirds World'. This search is still under way. It could have a profound effect on the direction of theological thinking in the 21st century.

At the same time it needs to be noted that there is still a considerable lack of enthusiasm within the WCC to grasp boldly and decisively the question of personal evangelism and its relationship to the church's involvement in strategies for social change. It is not enough for ecumenical leaders to point to the undoubtedly widespread evangelical resistance to political action. as if this justified their equally broad refusal to take seriously every person's individual need to be reconciled to God by means of Christ's death and resurrection alone. Neither should the idea that a changed society depends upon people being changed by this personal encounter with God be lightly set aside on the ground of its apparent origin in the individualistic presuppositions of a Western capitalist ideology.[27]

---

make persecution of Christians part of their policy. In Mozambique, the present government, formed from the ranks of Frelimo, is actively hostile to the churches, even when many Christians previously supported the independence struggle against Portugal. In Zimbabwe (Rhodesia), the Patriotic Front guerrillas have been quite indiscriminate in the targets they have chosen. No Christian theory of the 'just revolt' has ever justified the gratuitous massacre of non-combatants. In this case, many of them have been Christian missionaries themselves engaged in non-violent attempts to overcome racial prejudice and strife.

[26] The paper, 'Programme to Combat Racism' (cf. n. 17), says among other things: 'theological reflection by the Church on power as related to liberation and justice and its translation into action requires urgent attention.'

[27] While rejecting much of this ideology as being against the essential Christian values of compassion and justice, we need to call the Marxist bluff which pretends that Christian individualism has been determined wholly by a particular stage in the evolution of economic structures. On the contrary, Christian faith has also been responsible in part for a proper stress on the personal. Neither Marx nor Weber alone does justice to the interrelationship between ideas and

What is urgently needed both within ecumenical and conservative evangelical circles is a serious attempt to bring together theologically a concern both for social justice and for personal conversion. The setting up of a joint working-party whose terms of reference would be a thorough theological investigation of the inner relationship between the two,[28] and an analysis of those churches, groups and movements which appear in practice to be achieving a balance of both, might, in my view, be a positive way forward.

---

historical changes. Some notion of interaction between Christian belief and the social reality of man is the only way of doing justice to the totality of the facts of human existence. *Cf.* Robin Gill, *Theology and Social Structure* (London, 1977).

[28] In response to the 1980 Melbourne Conference of the Commission on World Mission and Evangelism, whose theme is 'Thy Kingdom Come', I have made a tentative attempt to do just this. *Cf.* J. A. Kirk, 'The Kingdom, the Church and a Distressed World', *The Churchman*, vol. 94, no. 2.

APPENDIX B

Violence:
business as usual?

There are probably many of us who in world terms veer towards pacifism, as there can be no just holocaust; and then feel the case for just rebellions in more limited contexts.
Michael Ramsey, 'Violence, Pacifism and Revolution',
Church of England Newspaper (3 March 1972).

If we succumb to the temptation to use violence in our struggle for freedom, the coming generations are destined to support a long and desolate night of bitterness and our principal legacy will be for them the unchangeable kingdom of chaos.
Martin Luther King, *The Trumpet of Conscience* (1967).

Most of us, by a quick association of ideas, connect revolution with violence. This is not surprising for revolution has been consistently linked with those political upheavals which have gained their ends through the use of superior force.

We ought not to assume, however, that revolution equals violent change. The question of violence goes beyond the issue of the violent overthrow of one order and the installation of another. It is also concerned naturally with the use of war as 'the continuation of the politics of the State by other means.' There is also the important question of the use of violence by individuals and small groups within society, not necessarily to gain control of the state but either to register some kind of political protest or simply to enrich themselves by armed robbery. In the case of vandalism and momentary physical assault, political and economic motives may be absent. Finally, there is the question of the state's 'legal' use of violence in the apprehension and punishment of law-breakers.

In general terms, then, violence may be seen in two ways: violence used *by* the state or *against* the state, and violence used *within* the state but without seeking to affect its policies. The first kind has been the concern of political scientists and the second of sociologists and psychiatrists. Both involve ethical questions of deep concern to the Christian conscience.

In the context of a theological appreciation of revolution, our interest centres on the first kind of violence and in particular the questions of war and revolt.

Varieties of violence

Violence is not mainly a theoretical issue. Scarcely any period of history has been free from war between nations. In the modern world we witness the calculated use of kidnapping, assassination and campaigns of terror to procure specific political ends. Many countries are subjected to regular *coups d'état*, which may well cause bloodshed among the civilian population.

In thinking about violence, this overt use of force to impose one's will on another comes readily to mind. But violence can also be covert, for it is any act by which the rights and freedom of another are violated by a system which possesses the means to enforce its will.

In this latter sense, much has been said in recent years about different forms of institutional violence. By this is meant the state's denial of elementary human rights. If, for example, an economic system is so managed that there is a permanent income imbalance between a small group of rich and a large group of poor (as is the case in our modern world), then violence is being committed against the dignity of human beings by denying them certain basic human requirements: a balanced diet, medical assistance, living conditions which protect against disease and the climate, equal educational opportunities, *etc.* Another important aspect of institutionalized violence is the lack of proper participation in decision-making processes affecting one's own future. This type of violence is most obvious in totalitarian, bureaucratically controlled or racist societies. More subtly, it is also present in the management of industry, when the employee is no more than a worker hired to carry out the production plans of the employer. It may also be present in the tendency in modern society to concentrate the means of production in giant multinational corporations, making entrepreneurial initiative on a small scale almost impossible.[1] Concentration may be justified either ideologically (socialist states) or on the grounds of economic efficiency (capitalism).

No discussion of violence is complete unless it considers this institutional violence, which Helder Camara calls 'the first violence'. Nevertheless, for reasons of space, we shall have to limit our discussion to overt political violence, used either by or against the state.

Violence and the state

Many have pointed out that violence is the logic of the state. Thoreau, for example, argued that a permanent army is simply the arm of a permanent government.[2] Clearly a state exists because it commands a greater amount of potential violence. Its armed forces exist not only to repel possible external aggression but also internal aggression used against it by any of its citizens, such as urban guerrillas.

The state's use of violence is ultimately sanctioned by the consent of the governed, who allow it to be used to protect their personal and property rights or to maintain a certain measure of internal order. There exists a long tradition in Christian thinking which maintains that violence may be delegated and used vicariously by the governing authorities on the theory that it is used 'to execute (controlled) wrath on the wrongdoer' (Rom. 13:4). In this sense the competent authorities, in order to restrain an arbitrary private use of violence, must have a monopoly of force in the nation.

However, the state's use of violence to protect some citizens against others can be extended to impose a particular ideology, or way of life, upon an unwilling population. This happens particularly when there are no ready-made, non-violent mechanisms (such as elections or referendums) for deposing the ruling group. In this case, self-perpetuating oligarchies, with the support or acquiescence of the

---

[1] *Cf.* the mammoth and minutely documented study by Richard J. Barnet and Ronald E. Muller, *Global Reach: The Power of the Multi-National Corporations* (New York, 1974). The presence of institutional violence is a topic in itself which deserves a separate study of its own.

[2] In his essay, 'Civil Disobedience'. The text can be found in *The Quiet Battle, Writings on the Theory and Practice of Non-Violent Resistance* (New York, 1963).

armed forces, create a repressive political structure basically to serve their own interests.

The state has often tended to accord itself 'a divine vocation and mission, giving it the right to adopt lies, deceit and homicide whenever its security is threatened'.[3] This is a far cry from its existence to defend the legitimate freedoms of all. The move from a functionalist to an absolutist form of the state is sometimes barely perceptible, but the effects are psychologically and physically felt. When the state uses violence indiscriminately to suppress potential opposition and to silence all forms of non-violent dissent it has become fascist, irrespective of its particular ideological banner.

In the present century it was Mussolini who first introduced into his philosophy the idea of permanent violence. According to Philip Windsor,[4] this cult of violence, also used by Mao Tse Tung in his struggle for leadership and against bureaucracy during the Chinese Cultural Revolution, is justified philosophically as *the* necessary means to create a new society. Violence is the epitome of that *élan vital* which will engender a new type of man: Nietzsche's superman, who in his striving for nobility and self-assurance is 'beyond good and evil'.

The opposite of the use of violence by the state to maintain law and order, on whatever grounds of legitimation, is its use by anarchists. Anarchism became a popular political option in the last century under such leaders as Bakunin, Kropotkin and Malatesta. Its object is to destroy the structure of the modern state and introduce a society 'in which the class system has been abolished, property is held in common, people live in communes, economic life is run by producer and consumer co-operatives, all by mutual agreement and without any organised authority.'[5] Bakunin advocated violence to dismantle the state apparatus, and there have been waves of anarchist violence, particularly in the 1890s. However, there is also a long tradition of non-violent anarchism, going back to such utopian socialists as Saint-Simon and Sombart. In the years since World War II, anarchism has centred on protest against all forms of militarism. It believes that state violence in all its form derives from the state's illegitimate

[3] Jean-Marie Muller, *L'Evangile de la non-violence* (Paris, 1969), chapter 5.
[4] 'Why Violence?', *The Listener*, vol. 94, 1971, p. 185.
[5] Nicolas Walter, 'Anarchism', *The Listener*, vol. 91, 1968, p. 232.

interference in the pursuits of its members, and produces a 'chaos of order'.

Non-violent anarchist action involves, in principle, a total withdrawal of co-operation with the state; as Tolstoy put it:

> Why submit to people who are sinners? Why give them taxes when money will be used to keep me in slavery? Why vote, giving the agents of violence the appearance of legitimacy?[6]

It was Gandhi, in his theory of *Hind Swaraj,* or self-government, who claimed that a massive movement of non-violence would inevitably produce a different kind of society, for the existence of the state as a legalized coercive force would no longer be justifiable.

Gandhi's disciples, Vinoba and Ramamurti,[7] further elaborated the nature of the new society to be built on the non-violent settling of disputes. As the power of decision is transferred from minorities to the people themselves, formed into small autonomous geographical groups, so the rationale for the existence of the state will disappear. The process will proceed from limitation, through non-co-operation to elimination.

Marxism and Violence

Because most of the major revolutions of the 20th century have been Marxist-inspired, and have been achieved through violent upheaval, it is generally assumed that the Marxist view of revolution necessarily involves the use of violence.

As a matter of fact, the Fathers of Marxism were unsure about the place of violence in revolutionary change. Certainly there exist texts which seem to suggest the inevitable place of violence in the coming of socialism. The most famous speaks of violence as the 'midwife' which gives birth to a revolutionary order. At the end of the *Communist Manifesto,* Marx and Engels state that

> the Communists disdain to conceal their views and aims. They openly

---

[6] 'The Kingdom of God is within you', text taken from Gonzalo Arias, *La no-violencia, arma política* (Barcelona, 1976), p. 43.

[7] 'How the State will be Abolished', *Asian Reader,* Madras, December 1968.

145

declare that their ends can only be attained by the forcible overthrow of all existing social conditions.

Earlier they had declared that

we have traced the more or less veiled civil war, raging within existing society, up to the point where the war breaks out into open revolution, and where the violent overthrow of the bourgeoisie lays the foundation for the sway of the proletariat.

Nevertheless, they did not develop any general theory of revolutionary violence, because they believed, on the presumed basis of empirical investigation, that the old order would collapse without the need of external provocation. The symbols of midwife and surgeon's scalpel, which speak of the birth of the new, are not so frequent as that of the grave-digger which speaks of the burial of the old:

the development of Modern Industry cuts from under its feet the very foundation on which the bourgeoisie produces and appropriates products. What the bourgeoisie, therefore, produces, above all, is its own grave-diggers.

Both men, therefore, were scathing in their denunciation of organized violence when this was designed to provoke rather than accompany the death throes of capitalist society.[8] Not that either of them had scruples about the use of violence, but they considered it only a tactical weapon, for only the development of particular economic forces would allow the proletariat to overthrow bourgeois society. They did not even believe that violence was absolutely necessary for this to happen.[9]

Marx's and Engels' basic belief in the spontaneity of revolution (also shared by Kautsky), accompanied or not by violence, was changed by the theory and practice of Lenin. Lenin used organized violence to provoke revolution though, paradoxically, the October

[8] For example, Marx, *Review of A. Chenu, The Conspirators* (Paris, 1850); Engels, *The Tactics of Social Democracy: Introduction to Marx's 'The Class Struggles in France, 1848–50'* (1895).

[9] Marx, *Speech at Amsterdam* (1872).

1917 Revolution was accomplished with hardly any bloodshed.[10]

Lenin's revolutionary strategy owed much to the late 19th-century Russian populist leaders, who proclaimed a general uprising of the peasant class against Tsarist despotism. Though he was formally a Marxist, and they were not, he came to adopt their political strategy which 'envisaged a victorious popular uprising and the seizure of power by the radical wing of the revolutionary movement.'[11] Whereas they stressed the popular uprising as the motor for revolutionary change, Lenin organized his Bolshevik party in such a way that it could take advantage of peasant (and bourgeois) opposition to the old order to plant itself in power. Meanwhile, the Mensheviks (the more orthodox Marxists) firmly believed that conditions in Russia in 1917 were not ripe for revolution. They believed that Lenin's tactics owed more to the Jacobin theory of conspiracy than to Marx's and Engels' expectation that wage labourers would achieve power through the disintegration of capitalist society.

Lenin's transformation of Marx in 'the organisation of "professional revolutionaries", which on the morrow of its victory transforms itself into the nucleus of a new ruling élite, is a 20th-century phenomenon.'[12] From there a straight line can be drawn to Ho Chi Minh, Fidel Castro, Samora Machel, Agostinho Neto, the Tupumaros and the Red Brigades.

Their legitimation of violence was no longer based on the (Hegelian) laws of historical development, but on the (medieval) logic of the 'just revolt'. This logic springs from the theory of the 'just war', and is dependent on the meaning given to tyranny in medieval doctrine. In contemporary revolutionary theory it is embellished by appeal to the Marxist notion of economic and political oppression.

The just-war theory

The Christian church's active support of war in certain circumstances was theologically defended in its most systematic form by Aquinas. He devised certain criteria by which the legitimacy, or otherwise, of a particular act of armed aggression could be measured.

His criteria can be conveniently grouped under four headings:

---

[10] N. F. Cantor, *The Age of Protest* (London, 1970), pp. 79–84.
[11] G. Lichtheim, *Marxism* (London, 1964), p. 347.   [12] *Ibid.*, p. 358.

(a) The cause must be just. This means that it will be fought only in self-defence, or in defence of other people, and in response to a calculated act of unprovoked aggression. However, the justification may be extended to include a pre-emptive strike when there is over-whelming evidence that the aggressor intends to attack. It must be the last resort when the belligerent refuses to settle differences by peaceful negotiations. Finally, the righteous cause must be reason-ably assured of victory.

(b) The intention must be good. Objectively, this means that the defending power resolves to restore peace as soon as possible. This peace must bring into being a more just order than existed before. Subjectively, it means that both the rulers who declare war and the soldiers who fight it must be governed by pure motives and not by desires for vengeance.

(c) The means used must be legitimate. Here, the aggrieved party has to apply the law of proportion, balancing the devastation and loss of life caused by the war against the good results gained by the war. In other words, the results of victory must be worth the amount of suffering and disruption of life needed to achieve it. A just war cannot involve innocent civilians, nor can it use methods which are intrinsically wrong. Finally, the terms must be equitable, the victo-rious power being ready to help repair the damage caused by the war on both sides. Lasting reconciliation and stability should be the prime aims of the victorious side.

(d) The war must be declared and fought by the legitimate author-ity. Not everyone has the right to go to war.

With the exception of this last criterion, these principles were also applied to the case of the 'just rebellion': the use of armed violence to overthrow a tyrannical government. Tyranny may be defined as the absolute and arbitrary use of power against the needs and wishes of the majority of the population. Modern revolutionary violence, though dressed up in a different ideological garb, is based on the logic of the just rebellion.

The medieval just-war theory had a long antecedent history. The Greeks and Romans took war for granted as a means either of spreading a superior civilization or maintaining a relatively more peaceful and stable society. More important for Christian thought was the Old Testament 'holy war' which seemed to provide a divine sanction for war in cases where true faith was being threatened.

Augustine in his reluctant defence of Christian participation in war appealed to both the Old Testament principle of defence of the faith, and the pagan-based defence of civilization and order.[13] After the Constantinian conversion of the state to Christianity, Christian faith and pagan civilization were joined in the concept of Christian civilization. Such a civilization needed, at least, defending against barbarism, even if its extension by the sword could not be legitimized.

However, Augustine also attacked war as a means of promoting Christian spiritual values and never justified its use on the basis of 'legitimate self-defence'. At this stage the church did not yet possess a developed basis for sanctioning active involvement in war. However, the new reality after Constantine forced it to seek a different set of ethical criteria, which responsible Christian rulers could apply within the limits imposed by a violent and unjust world.

In the 3rd century writers like Tertullian, Origen and Cyprian still maintained that arms-bearing was prohibited. But in the 4th century first its inevitability and then its conditional legitimacy were tentatively accepted.

In Christian thinking the just-war theory has been carefully distinguished from the secular doctrine of 'the Reason of State' which argues that the ruling power constitutes an autonomous authority competent to evolve its own criteria (such as the nebulous and arbitrary doctrine of national security) for the prosecution of wars. Christian thinking has never allowed the state tacitly to reject the control of God's law upon its actions. In the desire for autonomy, most notable in the 20th-century Fascist state, the idolatric tendency to use power in an unrestricted and unaccountable way becomes evident.

The church, although not very consistently, has also rejected the holy war, or crusade. The holy war rejects three of the just war criteria. Firstly, because of confidence in divine help even against overwhelming odds, and because martyrdom comes to be seen as a value in itself, the probability of victory as a necessary condition is qualified. Secondly, the criterion of justice is redefined in terms of

---

[13] *Cf.* Stanley Windass, *Christianity versus Violence* (London, 1964).

the 'spiritual' need to promote an absolutely worthy cause, and the more sober political terms are abandoned. Thirdly, because the enemy are cursed unbelievers, are less than human and their extermination is willed by God, the means employed are justified on strategic rather than moral grounds. Though theoretically rejected by Christian teaching, each one of these criteria of the holy war has been redefined in the modern defence of revolutionary violence, using messianic-secular rather than religious terms.

However, the just-war theory, at least until recent years, has been defended by the majority of Christian ethicists, both Roman Catholic and Protestant. In modern times its most consistent defender was Reinhold Niebuhr.[14] His theological defence of the theory begins from the reality of universal sin which pervades and destroys every human relationship. Sin introduces an inevitable element of conflict into the world which makes the attainment of relative (or equal) justice possible only by means of a certain degree of coercion, or by resistance to coercion and tyranny.

Though non-resistance may be the ideal to which the gospel points, it cannot deal with the day to day need to defend a relatively just order (democracy), or the life or property of defenceless and innocent people against the forces of anarchy, tyranny and injustice, potentially present in all human beings.

Niebuhr's argument is based on both theological and pragmatic assumptions. He argues that, though 'the ethic of Jesus is finally and ultimately normative,' it is not applicable now to the task of securing justice in a sinful world. This is because 'the ethic of the Kingdom,' in which no concession is made to human sin, is of a different order from 'all relative political strategies which, assuming human sinfulness, seek to secure the highest measure of peace and justice among selfish and sinful men.' Jesus' ethic is eschatological, the ideal which helps to discriminate between opposing claims of justice. It cannot, however, be relevant to human struggles in a non-Christian world, where we are often forced to choose between the lesser of two evils, neither of which really expresses the will of God. 'The significance of the law of love is precisely that it is not just another law but a law which transcends all law.' Meanwhile law, and its sanction in force,

---

[14] 'Why the Christian Church is not Pacifist' in *Christianity and Power Politics* (New York, 1940).

is necessary for those who do not accept the gospel.

Preventing the destruction of life against the unjust claims of an aggressor involves the exercising of a balance of power. This may be inferior to the harmony of love, but in its absence love becomes a screen which hides and condones injustice. 'When men suffer from anarchy (war), they foolishly regard the evils of tyranny as the lesser evils.'

The pacifist who benefits by a society in which coercion is the norm cannot arbitrarily introduce the uncompromising ethic of the gospel into one issue. Why, asks Niebuhr, should war be more offensive to Christian conscience than any other corporate evil? The pacifist fails to recognize that political controversies are conflicts between sinful men. So, in a world of sin, the establishing of justice can never be entirely free from vindictiveness.

> There is a point where the final cause of a criminal's anti-social conduct becomes fairly irrelevant in comparison with the task of preventing him from injuring innocent fellow-humans.

In this quotation the just-war theory is based on a logical extension of the right of competent authorities to restrain evil within their own territories. War is rationalized as a kind of extra-territorial policing act. The logic of the argument may have some validity where formal defence treaties exist between states, based on the right of armed intervention in any case of naked aggression. However, the argument is really very weak for a number of other reasons. Firstly, it depends for its validity on being able to establish who are the authorities competent to exercise violence on a world scale. Ultimately, to restrain criminals and to declare war on another sovereign state are acts of a qualitatively different order, for no country can set itself up as both defendant and judge of its own cause. But where is the world authority which can declare particular wars just or unjust? Moreover, there can be no way of gaining redress against war except by war. There is no international mechanism for enforcing decisions upon individual states except by war. Finally, a wholly consistent application of the just-war theory demands that any one should be willing to fight against his own country if he is convinced that the opponent's cause is more just than his own. This should be the radical test of the sincerity of the theory. However, it is precisely here that the abstract and unrealistic nature of the whole theory manifests itself. How can anyone establish which side represents the just cause when both sides control the means of propaganda? Or who can be rationally cool enough to disengage himself from the passions of nationalism? In the last analysis the defence of war is quite romantic, for it discounts the ambiguity of all events which lead up to war.

The meaning of non-violence

A considerable body of people down the ages have refused to defend the use of any kind of coercive force, even as a last resort (*ultima ratio*), as a means of solving social and political problems.

Non-violence may take several forms. In the case of the Quakers it has meant the rejection of all recourse to physical restraint. It may simply involve the rejection of war (usually referred to as pacifism), while admitting the legitimacy of an internal police force. It may imply a totally passive response to all covert and overt violent pro-vocation through withdrawal from society (as in the case of the Jehovah's Witnesses), or it may involve concerted action to change situations by means which do not involve physical abuse.

It is in this latter sense that non-violence has, in the last thirty years or so, become an attractive alternative political and social strategy for both Christians and non-Christians alike. John Swomley defines it as:

> direct, effective and organised action against forms of injustice and aggression, which shows respect for the physical integrity of those it opposes, while at the same time attempting to eliminate the injustice or oppression they are producing.[15]

It implies a deliberate policy of non-cooperation or disobedience to those authorities which either demand a commitment to evil action or deliberately maintain unjust structures in existence.

Like the defence of limited violence, it possesses both a theological

[15] Definition in an unpublished paper on 'Violence and Revolution' (Buenos Aires, 1969). For a fuller treatment by him of the subject *cf.* J. Swomley, *Liberation Ethics: a Political Scientist Examines the Role of Violence in Revolutionary Change* (New York, 1972).

and a pragmatic rationale. Christians appeal to the teaching and life-style of Jesus and the early Christian church as sufficient evidence that violence is never a legitimate response to violence. In this sense they believe that Christ's Kingdom ethic is not only relevant to life in a lost world but also mandatory. G. H. C. Macgregor argues[16] that 'Jesus makes his characteristic demands not in view of an immediate end of the present age, but on the ground that such a way of life is alone consistent with God's nature.' In other words, Jesus' ethic cannot be postponed to the future, while in the present we make decisions on the basis of a 'prudential ethic for present realities.'

Moreover, it is clear from Jesus' own action that he believed that non-violence was a clear political option, not bound by the false dichotomy between repressive and revolutionary violence on the one hand, or complete non-involvement on the other. Macgregor, J. H. Yoder[17] and others accuse those who maintain that Jesus was not involved in the relativities of politics of a 'complete misreading of the historical situation of the Gospels'. Macgregor argues that in view of Jesus' claim to be the Messiah, the injunction to the messianic community to 'love its enemies' must have applied to the contemporary political situation. Yoder has developed the thesis that Christ's non-violent stance was an alternative strategy of socio-political commitment, not so much to the structural violence of the Herodians, Sadducees and Romans, as to the 'just' revolutionary violence of the Zealots.

Those Christians who reject a legitimate recourse to violence differ radically from other Christians on the application of Jesus' ethic. For them it is not simply a paradigm, but a universal commandment, and for two reasons. First, the problem of violence goes to the heart of the question of how God will bring in a new order. The often adduced analogy of divorce, where we are confronted both with an ideal and with possible exceptions, is a false analogy because it belongs to a different level of reality. There can be no exception to

the ideal of non-violence, because it is an integral part of the meaning of Christ's redemption on the cross and, by implication, of the call to the

[16] G. H. C. Macgregor, *The Relevance of an Impossible Ideal* (New York 1960), p. 138.
[17] Mostly notably in J. H. Yoder, *The Politics of Jesus* (Grand Rapids, 1972).

153

Christ's redemption on the cross and, by implication, of the call to the disciple to 'take up his cross daily and follow Christ'.[18]

In this sense non-violence may be understood as a sacramental act of the gospel; through it the mystery of redemptive suffering is proclaimed 'until he comes'.

Second, the distinction made between the ideal and the real in Jesus' ethic introduces into Christian thought and practice a disastrous moral dualism. A dichotomy is made, firstly, between personal and collective morality (Jesus teaches nothing about how to realize political ends); secondly, between intention and action (God is primarily concerned about our inner disposition); thirdly, between norms applicable to Christians and those applicable to non-Christians (God cannot expect or require non-violence from unregenerate, fallen man); and fourthly between a Christian's responsibility in public office (the Christian ruler or soldier) and in private life. From the 4th century onwards, this double morality was institutionalized in the form of monasticism: the Christian who could not accept the double standard in ordinary life was encouraged to withdraw from the world!

Pragmatically, non-violence, like violence, is a means to achieve a given end, but there are two essential differences between them. The one relates to the effectiveness of either method for combating violence and injustice; the other concerns the relative, or absolute importance given to the means used. In the latter case the advocates of non-violence reject the argument of the lesser evil because it depends ultimately on the premise that any evil is legitimate if used as a remedy for anything more evil than itself. The danger of the argument lies in the fact that those who justify their use of violence, by appealing to the superior moral quality of the cause they defend, are bound to exaggerate the beneficial ends which will be achieved by violence, and so minimize the adverse consequences of the means employed. This is why many feel that non-violent action which forbids physical coercion, especially killing, is a more, not less, realistic response to man's essential corruption; for it does not have to resort to the kind of special pleading involved in the just-war

---

[18] 'Violence/Non-violence', paper prepared by J. H. Yoder for a seminar held in Buenos Aires, September-October, 1970.

theory. It is also free from the whole casuistic process of balancing relative justice against possible consequences.

The strategic value of a policy of non-violent action is based on the observed fact that no authority can govern except by the consent of the people. Remove that consent and change is inevitable. Violence possesses no monopoly of power, for if power is 'the ability to accomplish purpose',[19] violence is clearly not indispensable to its exercise.

In reality power is not defined by violence. Violence is the instrument of a kind of power, but 'the ultimate form of power is . . . the solidarity of a people committed tenaciously to a common purpose.'[20] Power through violence can be exercised by a disproportionately small number of people using superior weapons;[21] but continuing power depends on the collaboration, or at least indifference, of the majority.[22] This is why strategies of non-violence have to co-ordinate a large, disciplined group of people to struggle for a common end. On the other hand, if rulers begin to lose their power-base in society, they must increase their use of violence proportionately in order to survive. In these circumstances the effectiveness of violence is based on its ability to violate the human dignity of the majority. Power, however, can be exercised only with the active or tacit consent of the majority. As Jean-Marie Muller says, non-violent action 'aspires to take power, not *for* the people, but *by* the people.'[23]

Lack of space forces me to omit more arguments in favour of the strategic value and redemptive character of non-violence. However, we do not want to leave the subject without pointing out some serious misunderstandings of the non-violent position often made by otherwise serious students of revolution and violence. For example, J. G. Davies[24] makes several false assumptions, rather typical of those who adopt the traditional Christian defence of the just war:

---

[19] Swomley, *Liberation Ethics*, p. 63.   [20] *Ibid.*, p. 64.

[21] The frightening possibility that terrorist groups may soon acquire the use of atomic weapons looms on the horizon of future political strategy. It is difficult to see how such an occurrence could be eliminated by any kind of balance of tactical weaponry, such as has occured between the super-powers.

[22] H. Arendt, *On Violence* (London, 1970) devotes a chapter to demonstrating the real source of political power, pp. 33–36.   [23] *L'évangile de la non-violence.*

[24] J. G. Davies, *Christians, Politics and Violent Revolution* (London, 1976), chapter 6, 'Violence', pp. 121–187.

(a) Jesus' ethic cannot be disregarded simply out of fear of its becoming a new legalism. In fact it rejects the old righteousness of the law, but only in order to establish the righteousness of the new age. It is a concrete manifestation of the law of love. How else is love to be known as such, if not in the action of a concrete person? Or, how is the Kingdom operative for Davies *now*, if he can justify force on grounds which are not specifically Christian in content?

(b) To state that Jesus' choices were wholly different from ours means ignoring his political context. There is a sense in which the cross is a unique act of universal salvation; and there is another sense in which the Christian can share in its significance ('take up his cross daily'). As the result of a deliberate choice to renounce a particular way of exercising power, the cross is directly relevant to the means chosen to effect political change.

(c) Davies (almost) confuses pacifism with passivity. He establishes a wholly false antithesis between the use of force and the promotion of change. The issue between force and non-violence is not over how a particular reality should be interpreted (where tyranny exists), nor over what ends are desirable, but over means. The 'pacifist' believes that the change brought about by force cannot be genuine revolutionary change, merely an exchange of those people and ideologies which control the state.

(d) The just-war theory grew out of a Christian consensus. Because this no longer exists in the modern world, its value is conjectural. The arguments used to support it today bear little relation to real historical circumstances: the use of violence in Angola (p. 163) did not lead to 'embraces and fraternization' but to civil war. In Cuba we must take into account not just the armed revolt against Batista (p. 178), but the subsequent violence of Castro's regime (compare Russia in 1917 and Stalin's reign of terror). If Davies had actually lived through an era of major guerrilla warfare (such as in Argentina from 1969–1977) he might modify his statement that 'threats and terror are not their normal weapons *vis-à-vis* the population as a whole.' (p. 176).

(e) There is no historical evidence for maintaining that non-violence could be successful only within the norms of a democratic society (p. 164), for it has rarely been tried as a tactic in a totalitarian state (but what about Denmark and Norway under Nazism, and El

Salvador in 1944?). One major problem with justified force is that when circumstances do not permit its use (*i.e.*, when there is no reasonable chance of success), there remains no strategy for change. This, in my view, is one of the great weaknesses of movements of resistance to right-wing military dictatorships in Latin America. There has been little tradition of creative non-violent movements for change (Helder Camara is an exception which probably proves the rule), but there might be immense possibilities for this course of action in different Latin American situations.

These and other arguments reveal the kind of special pleading which exponents of the just war theory are forced to make if they wish to apply the theory today. It is a pity that Davies seems not to have studied the work of representatives of non-violence like Swomley and Yoder, for he has done their position little justice.

How do we decide?

The foregoing discussion has tried to highlight some of the complex issues thrown up by the reality and cult of violence. In summarizing our findings we shall try to pinpoint some of the basic issues which should shape our own conclusions on the subject.

Basically, Christians come to different conclusions because they attach importance to different starting points. Those who oppose any legitimation of violence accord overriding importance to the absolute nature of Jesus' ethic. As Yoder puts it,

> to say that the Sermon on the Mount is not legalistically binding gives no grounds for saying that a Christian should, in an extreme case, do just the contrary of what is there 'directed'. We must hear a firm counter-imperative.[25]

Those who defend violence as an *ultima ratio* tend to begin from a general theological maxim about the nature of man and the world. Niebuhr assumes that the depravity of man must be checked and balanced by the use of physical force. Barth assumes that the forcible defence of an imperfect way of life is better than capitulation to one which totally and flagrantly defies God's will for man; Switzerland

[25] J. H. Yoder, *Karl Barth and the Problem of War* (Philadelphia, 1970), p. 59.

was well prepared for armed resistance if necessary against Nazi Germany.

These different starting points imply different ways of reading the Scriptures. This is partly a question of interpretation and partly one of hermeneutics. The question of interpretation involves the relative importance given to certain biblical themes in applying the biblical message to the choice between violence and non-violence. Those who charge that the rejection of all violence is 'heresy' usually maintain that, in dealing with the unrighteous action of a non-Christian, the principle of the righteousness of God's law must be applied. A man cannot properly hear the gospel till he understands the sanctions of the law. Sometimes he will admit that good and evil are part of a moral universe and not man's invention, only when he feels the force of violence in curbing his inclination towards evil. On the other side, it is pointed out that though law precedes the gospel, 'because of transgressions', God's promise of mercy and salvation precedes the law, and holds out hope precisely for those who cannot fulfil the law. The gospel, in fulfilling the promise, sets forth a new law of non-retaliatory love which replaces the old law of proportionate retaliation.

The hermeneutical question follows from certain implications of biblical interpretation. It really concerns the theological and existential fact that a person in Christ is simultaneously involved in two realities: the old age of Adam and the new age of Christ's resurrection life. The justice achieved throught the sanctions of the law is not the justice achieved through a voluntary acceptance of the law of love made possible in the gospel. The fundamental question, then, is whether the Christian should seek to implement both kinds of justice or only the second kind. Does the Christian have simultaneous, though distinct, responsibilities to the two orders, or does he have an exclusive commitment to the new order which then has to be applied within the conditions of the old? For Barth, the implication of denying all violence is to deny the legitimacy of the state. For Yoder, the only way of taking the state's function seriously is by consistently exposing its facility for justifying its own violence. One says that the defence of a state dedicated to justice, or the overthrow of a totally unjust state, is ultimately more important than the cost of all the lives which such action will entail. The other says that it is impossible to make this kind of judgment, so on ethical grounds derived from the New Testament he refuses to give the benefit of the doubt either to the state or to the revolutionaries.

The application of biblical teaching to contemporary problems of violence leads us to consider the logic of the 'lesser evil'. It is generally agreed that the burden of proof for the right of legitimate defence falls on those who defend violence. The just-war theory, then, is simply meant to limit and circumscribe violence. The fundamental principle adduced for supporting particular instances of violence is usually that of the lesser evil. The argument is that in some circumstances a policy of non-violence brings more evil consequences than one of limited violence (*e.g.* in peaceful mass demonstrations against brutal totalitarian governments more people may be killed than in prolonged guerrilla warfare). The advocate of non-violence says that the taking of life can never be the lesser of two evils and that the only alternative to war or guerrilla warfare need not be mass demonstrations, however peaceful. So the logic of the lesser evil is itself refused, for if there is a third choice the lesser evil may be the second best of three possibilities, and therefore wrong.

Different kinds of non-violent action according to local circumstances constitute this third choice between violence and acquiescence. This seems to be how Christ revealed God's will for the people of the new age. In practice it has shown itself to be the only way of achieving real justice, equality and reconciliation, the aim of all methods designed to change inhuman and threatening situations.

Finally, the question arises whether total abstention from all forms of physical coercion is really a practical proposition. Many Christians, who are either opposed to all war on principle, or who now believe that the threat of nuclear and biological warfare has made the whole just-war and just-rebellion theory completely inoperable and irrelevant (nothing more than a theoretical nicety),[26] would nevertheless support the need for police to enforce the law. Muller, for example, believes that police are necessary to defend the legitimate freedom of everyone. André Dumas argues that 'it is not a question of trying to disarm the violence of another through generosity, but

---

[26] When a particular means is used to wage war which involves uncontrollable, mass destruction of life, the principle of proportionate justice is quite incalculable, *cf.* Oliver O'Donovan, 'The Just War Theory in Recent American Writing', *The Churchman*, 86, 3, 1972.

restricting the other's evil through violence.'[27]

The pacifist can refuse to participate in war and revolutionary war. But consistently to refuse support to a police force, he must withhold a portion of his income tax and reject all physical protection for himself. Here we reach, perhaps, the limit-point between life in the two ages.

[27] 'Biblia y violencia' in P. Dabezies *et al.*, *Teología de la violencia* (Salamanca, 1971), p. 22; *cf.* also Richard B. Gregg, *The Power of Non-violence* (London, 1960), chapter 8.

PART III

Where do we go from here?

Chapter Nine

Is there revolution in revelation?

But according to his promise we wait for new heavens and a new earth in which righteousness dwells.

2 Peter 3:13

The main part of our analysis of contemporary revolutionary theology is over. It is clear that whatever geographical, ideological or doctrinal differences may exist between them, an increasing number of theological thinkers from a variety of backgrounds are convinced that theological reflection upon current (and future) models of revolution must go on. I agree wholeheartedly with this judgment because, if for no other reason, revolutionary change is likely to be an increasing part of the experience of Christians everywhere. This means that the church cannot fulfil the mission Jesus Christ has sent her to accomplish unless she understands the varied meanings and implications of revolution.

Theology's encounter with revolution is still only in its initial stages. Outside of a minority of Christian leaders in the Third World and the Western churches, little serious thinking about revolution has been undertaken. Christians who identify themselves with historical evangelical convictions are still largely unaware of the urgency of the discussion. If the issues we have been reviewing in the preceding chapters have any relevance to life in general, those with theological expertise must be willing to devote more time to looking closely at the questions which have been raised.

If the message of Scripture is to have a critical, controlling role in one's theological assessment of revolution, we have to find a method of interpretation which allows the text to speak directly to the revolutionary situations envisaged. Given our previous lack of concern, as Christians, with the challenge of revolution, this method will have to be experimental. To prejudge conclusions at this particular junc-

163

ture would seem to me the height of arrogance, for at present there is no single orthodox understanding of how biblical truth relates to political and social revolution.

In this chapter we shall give some examples of how this kind of interpretation might be undertaken. Not too much should be expected of them, for they are no more than preliminary attempts to look at some of the evidence. Indeed, those of us who believe in the complete authority and trustworthiness of the Bible must realize that our approach to the text, based on the willingness to hear and obey, never automatically implies that we have found an infallible way of understanding its meaning. Dogmatic certainty in the realm of interpretation, particularly on a subject as unresearched as this, may be a sign of sheer Christian immaturity.

Our purpose, then, is to select those events in the history of salvation which, in the light of our whole discussion, appear to have some relevance to the question of revolution. Without neglecting the validity and importance of classical methods of biblical interpretation, we shall especially need to adopt a hermeneutical approach to the Bible. In other words, we must seek to draw out and then test all possible aspects of its significance for revolutionary issues. We shall find that these issues pose fresh questions about the text which will challenge us to find new firm principles for belief and action, so that we can hear correctly what the Holy Spirit is saying to the churches today.[1]

Careful hermeneutics does not try to foreclose the discussion about the way in which the Bible should be interpreted and applied in different circumstances. Thus, for example, we may well find that our view of how the message of the Bible relates to revolution may look very different according to whether or not we have been personally confronted by revolution. The way in which Scripture is to be understood is a practical question which cannot be settled by theoretical discussion. Whether or not we have succeeded in allowing the text to speak in an authentic way, one which maintains the supremacy of Jesus Christ over every political ideology and movement for social, cultural and ethical change, will have to be decided in retrospect. Biblical hermeneutics demands a certain amount of

[1] I have tried to give a coherent account of my view of biblical hermeneutics in 'The Use of the Bible in Interpreting Salvation Today', *Evangelical Review of Theology*, I 1 (November 1977).

trial and error, the willingness to have our ideas and actions altered by a more convincing interpretation of Scripture than the one we have adopted hitherto.

Particularly in areas of the world where there are great political unheavals and tension, the practical necessity of deciding to what extent the Bible supports or questions modern revolutionary theory and practice urges us to press on with this task, consciously accepting the risks which may be involved.

The question of world-views

As Lenin once remarked, 'every revolutionary practice needs a revolutionary theory.' And, we might add, every revolutionary theory is dependent upon a general view of man and history. In other words, to be coherent and lasting, revolutionary motivation must be based on something much deeper than a strictly political drive for power.

All great revolutionary thinkers have realized this. Marx, for example, despite the disclaimers of orthodox Communist theoreticians, did not derive his revolutionary convictions from a totally objective, aseptic, empirical study of history. Before he advanced his most characteristic themes – the class struggle, the inevitable collapse of capitalism and the dictatorship of the proletariat – he had already imbibed Hegel's philosophical interpretation of world history: *i.e.* progress through the resolution of contradictions and a final synthesis of antagonistic forces in a realm of true liberty for mankind. Into Hegel's framework Marx fitted both his analysis of man's alienation and the concept of the proletariat as the harbinger of a new age.[2]

Does the Bible also possess a revolutionary theory? Does it contain a coherent world-view which can be applied, more or less directly, to today's revolutionary ferment? These questions are not purely hypothetical, for many Christians have, in fact, found biblical support and inspiration for their revolutionary programmes.

The following elements of biblical faith seem to me to form a world-view which, compared with forces that simply conserve or paralyse ideas and structures, has definite revolutionary overtones:

[2] *Cf.* Paul-Dominique Dognin, *Initiation à Karl Marx* (Paris, 1970).

(a) God's action in the world has caused a mythological, naturalistic and cyclical view of reality to give way to a linear, historical view. God is neither the prime mover of all things, nor the guarantor of an unchangeable natural order. He is the God who reveals an eschatological purpose for man: the creation of a new kind of people. This new creation presupposes a process of change advancing steadily towards final consummation.

(b) In order to bring salvation to man, God wages an unremitting struggle against the representatives (idols) of alternative world-views. Thus, for example, the gods of Egypt were the guarantors of a theocratic order in which power was invested in a priestly caste. They combined responsibility for maintaining the natural order intact against the perennial threat of chaos with the privilege of being the main owers of wealth. The people of Israel after liberation from Egypt were organized according to a radically different model, corresponding to a different view of God and the universe.

(c) In the mythical world-view salvation implies security against the threat of uncontrollable natural forces. In biblical perspective it implies rescue from a moral rebellion against God's truth about the world he has created. Non-biblical cosmologies are based on a non-moral reading of reality: actions are judged favourably, if they promote the stability of an already existing, sacred order. In this sense justice and injustice, oppression and exploitation, would be strictly meaningless categories, for there is no concept of a God who can say, 'The voice of your brother's blood is crying to me from the ground' (Gn. 4:10).

(d) Finally, God's purpose of salvation is globally summed up in the promise of 'new heavens and a new earth in which righteousness dwells' (2 Pet. 3:13).

The premise here is that there is absolutely nothing sacred or final about the present created order. According to the promise God's activity is directed towards establishing a new creation which is qualitatively different from the existing one. Therefore, he repudiates every aspect of human life which contradicts the reality of the new order (the Kingdom) which he is creating (1 Cor. 6:9–10; Eph. 5:5; 2 Thes. 1:5–9; Rev. 21:4, 21–27). Being eschatological, the new order is intrinsically subversive of all existing structures and systems.

God's promise of a new created order puts all human achievements under the judgment of an eschatological absolute. In biblical perspective, man's existence is determined in an ultimate sense by the reality of the future.

Creation

No-one would disagree that the Bible teaches that every man is created in God's image. However, the precise significance of this idea is interpreted in different ways.

The doctrine of creation, for example, has often been used in Christian theology to support an intrinsically non-revolutionary view of man's place in the world. For example, the concept of different human 'orders' or 'spheres' of activity has tended to divide human life into separate compartments, granting substantial autonomy to each particular area of life.[3]

Such a view of creation seems to be closer to a deistic than a theistic belief. The former presupposes that the different 'orders' of human activity are given as part of an initial, all-embracing created structure of life. To fulfil these 'orders' means simply to unfold this original structure. The latter presupposes that, because creation is a continuing process of divine activity in which man, through his work, joins with his creator, new structures may constantly replace obsolete ones. In this sense, the mandate to subdue the world, as a co-operative human venture, is a revolutionary task. That is why the modern industrial state, which was born out of the application of new scientific discoveries, may justly be called a revolutionary event. Engels once said,

> Whilst in France the hurricane of the Revolution swept over the land, in England a quieter, but not on that account less tremendous, revolution was going on. Steam and the new tool-making machinery were transforming manufacture into modern industry and thus *revolutionising the whole foundation* of bourgeois society.[4]

[3] This is particularly true of the classical Lutheran doctrine of the 'two kingdoms', cf. H. Thielicke, *Theological Ethics, II: Politics* (London, 1969), pp. 1–21. Some developments of Reformed theological thinking (e.g., the 'Dooyeweerdian school') seem to come close to this position, cf. H. Dooyeweerd, *In the Twilight of Western Thought* (Philadelphia, 1960).

[4] Engels, 'Socialism: Utopian and Scientific' in R. C. Tucker (ed.) *Marx-Engels Reader* (New York, 1972). p. 612 (my italics).

Living one hundred years after Engels penned these words we are even better able to judge the revolutionary impact of technological progress upon human life.

The call of Abraham

The idea of historical destiny is strongly present in the story of Abraham: 'Go from your country and your kindred . . . to the land that I will show you. And I will make of you a great nation' (Gn. 12:1–2).

Abraham is presented in the Bible as the father of those who are convinced that God fulfils his promises (Jn. 8:39–40; Rom. 4:16–25; Gal. 3:7, 18; Heb. 11:8ff.). An attitude of confident trust in a God who makes history enables new beginnings to take place. If man simply believes in himself and his own capabilities, change will be insubstantial and ephemeral, but if he believes that the God of the nations is creating a new people to be a blessing for all humanity, he will expect many established patterns to be upset.

In part, Abraham's calling was to be the prototype of a pilgrim people whose life in the world is wholly encompassed by God's eschatological fulfilment of salvation history:

> He went out, not knowing where he was to go. By faith he sojourned in the land of promise, as in a foreign land, living in tents. . . . For he looked forward to the city which has foundations, whose builder and maker is God (Heb. 11:8–10).

The whole idea of the stability and security of a given order is shattered by the Abraham story. A tent does not have stable foundations. All that man creates is temporary and removable:

> 'Yet once more,' indicates the removal of what is shaken, as of what has been made, in order that what cannot be shaken may remain. Therefore, let us be grateful for receiving a kingdom that cannot be shaken . . . (Heb. 12:27–28).

Only the ultimate, the new order which God is preparing, cannot be changed.

168

The exodus

Israel's liberation from oppressive slavery in Egypt has been taken by revolutionary theology as the chief biblical paradigm for revolutionary change. Old Testament scholarship has generally assumed that Israel's history as a nation begins from this dramatic event. More particularly some theologians believe that, in the escape from Egypt, Israel achieved its own liberation from bondage, giving itself the freedom necessary to build a new kind of society.[5]

However, as the text stands at present, neither assumption is correct. Israel was already conscious of being a people, even before being subjected to slave-labour in the land of their adoption. To speak of the God of Abraham, Isaac and Jacob (Ex. 3:15–16; 4:5) is not simply a convention adopted by later chroniclers, for the people clearly possessed a strong memory of a God who had been with their fathers (*e.g.* Ex. 1:17), even if he now revealed himself to them in a new way (Ex. 6:2–3). The text also consistently proclaims that Israel's liberation is due to the initiative, direction and overwhelming power of God. Trying to identify one stratum of tradition which originally spoke of a self-liberation is an arbitrary procedure. It rests on the gratuitous assumption that some evidence of Moses as a national liberating hero must be present. Naturally, it is possible to bend the text to give some support for any theory. But in this case the approach simply betrays the philosophical, historical and ideological conditioning of those who use it.

This is not to deny that the Hebrews played some part in their liberation. In a real sense the process began when the midwives, in an act of civil disobedience, refused to co-operate in a policy of genocide (Ex. 1:17ff). Then, too, the cry for help (Ex. 2:23) was a positive refusal to accept a state of permanent oppression. The Hebrews rejected a fatalistic outlook on life and protested against an iniquitous system.

At the same time, the story makes it clear that the Hebrews were

---

[5] *Cf.* my discussion of the interpretation of the exodus by Liberation Theology in *Liberation Theology* (London, 1979).

[6] *Cf.* the discussion by R. de Vaux of the relevant passages in 'The Revelation of the Divine name YHWH' in *Proclamation and Presence: Old Testament Essays in Honour of G. H. Davies* (London, 1970).

not liberated simply because they were oppressed. There were other oppressed people of the time who were not liberated in this way. The Hebrews were rescued from bondage so that God could fulfil through one people a special mission for the world. The groaning reminds God (Ex. 2:24) that he had promised to establish this 'no-people' (Dt. 7:7–8) in a land where they would be free to acknowledge that he alone is God and to keep the laws of the covenant.

The exodus marks the theoretical and geographical separation between two societies. Egypt was a sacral society, sanctified by the presence of a holy caste. This society's proper functioning depended upon a minutely observed set of religious conventions. Israel was a sacred society, set apart by the God of world-history for a special task. Its proper functioning depended upon the abolition of every concept of caste.

The social laws

In establishing the rules to govern social life among this new people the Lord consistently appeals to the great act of liberation from Egypt: 'You shall not oppress a stranger; you know the heart of a stranger, for you were strangers in the land of Egypt' (Ex. 23:9; cf. 20:2).

The laws were based on God's character as a liberating God. Their negative function was to prevent exploitation (Ex. 22:25–27; Lv. 19:13; Dt. 24:7); while their positive function was to set wholly new standards for the meaning of life in community (for example, the outsider and the weak are given a specially privileged place in the new nation (Ex. 22:21–23; Dt. 10:17–19; 24:17–18)). Though the laws recognize the right of individual ownership, they also prevent individuals from accumulating great wealth for themselves. Thus the sabbatical and jubilee laws, by restoring property rights to former owners after a certain period of time, prevented the permanent creation of great differences of wealth among brethren.[7]

---

[7] Cf. R. de Vaux, *Ancient Israel: its Life and Institutions* (London, 1973), Part I: chapter 5; Part II: chapters 2, 3, 9, 11; R. Sider, *Rich Christians in an Age of Hunger* (Downers Grove, 1977), pp. 88–95. This latter book is a serious attempt to engage in a biblical hermeneutic meaningful to contemporary social issues.

Theocracy and monarchy

The laws governing the use of land, the main capital asset of an agricultural community, stem from the theological truth that man is steward, rather than owner, of God's creation (Ex. 19:5; Lv. 25:23). With the popular clamour for a king (1 Sa. 8:4–5), already refused by Gideon (Jdg. 8:22–23) on the grounds that Israel already has one and does not need another, the nation begins to forget this truth.

The price which Israel has to pay for greater national security is the centralization of both political power and economic wealth. This becomes particularly true in Solomon's reign when the bureaucratic control of the people, already begun under David, was consolidated.

Centralization, as Samuel had predicted (1 Sa. 8:11–18), leads to the private, or dynastic, accumulation of wealth through exploitation. It also leads to an unrestrained concentration of power, accountable to no-one.

The monarchy was based, once again, on the mythical world-view which held that a privileged minority had been granted a divine right to rule (1 Sa. 8:7–8; 10:18–19). But in the case of Israel such a right implies a return to the Egyptian model of government and a rejection of the alternative experience of the Lord's direct rule.

After the exile, leadership in Israel, as in the time of the judges, became again somewhat charismatic (for example, Nehemiah, the Maccabees). By the 1st century BC, however, it was oligarchic and self-perpetuating. The development during this period of a new dynasty, though somewhat weakened by the Roman occupation, led to an incredible series of intrigues and struggles for power, of which the people usually became the innocent victims.[8] Herod the Great's policy of constructing magnificent public works bears the same marks of demagogic grandeur from which not a few nations have suffered in recent years.[9]

The Old Testament obviously does not bear witness to the modern concept of democracy. Such an idea would be clearly anachronistic. Nevertheless, in the pre-monarchical and post-exilic periods it

[8] Josephus in *The Antiquities* and *The Jewish War* gives a wealth of details which, even if exaggerated, amount to a stunning exposé of brutality and corruption.

[9] Whatever the total evaluation of Perón's first period of rule in Argentina (1946–55), part of his extensive modernization of the country was due to demagogic motives.

describes a situation where the limits to individual and group power, basic to the proper functioning of democracy, are clearly visible (*cf.* Ne. 5:1ff.). In the modern period dynastic rule has been exercised by families (kings, emirates, *etc.*), by *the* party (Communist states), by the military (many Third World nations) and by racial minorities (South Africa). Democracy has broken up dynastic rule, showing up its unrepresentative and therefore ultimately arbitrary character. But it can function only where there is real regard for equality before the law (*cf.* Ex. 23:6–8 Lv. 19:15–16), and where the law itself is based on the twin principles of justice and compassion (Dt. 16:18–20; Dt. 21:15ff.; 23:15–16, 24–25; Is. 30:18, 61:8).

The prophetic voice

The prophets spoke their message to the royal court and the priests who exercised power and, therefore, responsibility for the nation. They were sent because the rulers brazenly oppressed the weak, exhibiting a total disregard for the social laws of the covenant (Is. 65:1–7; Je. 11:7–8; 34:8ff).

They were also sent because the Lord had compassion on his people. He gave them opportunity to repent and be restored, but also warned them of severe judgment if they thought he was not serious about social righteousness (Is. 58:6–12; 63:7–10).

Israel needed to be saved from its internal enemies: all those who abandoned allegiance to the God of liberation and ran instead after pagan Baalim. The prophets were concerned first with idolatry and then with injustice. The latter, though central to their message of judgment, was not so much the cause of Israel's sin as the result of their attitude towards God (Is. 2:5–11).

However, the promise of a new beginning for the nation was given in the very middle of the message of condemnation (Mi. 4:1–4, 6–8). Israel would again become a theocracy, but of a more intimate kind. God would rule his people through a prince of righteousness (Is. 11:4–5; 32:1, 16–17; Je. 23:6; 33:15) and through his Spirit (Is. 11:2; 61:1; Ezk. 36:26–27; 37:14). A new covenant would be based on the promise of an internal moral regeneration, deriving from a personal knowledge of God. This would then become the source of a renewal of righteousness among the people (Je. 31:31–4).

The desire of God's people to imitate the power structures of the surrounding nations had led to a catastrophic disaster, but through the suffering of an innocent minority, God would establish his true justice once again (Is. 42:1–4, 49:6–13; 53:3–12).

Jesus Christ and revolution

Whether we accept their entire thesis or not, the studies of Cullmann, Hengel, Brandon, Yoder and others,[10] have conclusively demonstrated that Jesus did not evade the revolutionary debate of his day. The real significance of the temptation narrative, for example, is lost unless we assume that the Zealot concept of the holy war is in the background.[11]

Jesus was clearly not a politician in the accepted sense of one seeking to use power to change society from the top downwards. His few recorded remarks about Herod show that he rejected this way of revolution (Lk. 7:25; 9:51–56; 13:31–32). Nevertheless, his whole ministry actively challenged, by both word and deed, the ideological rationalizations and political expediencies upon which societies are ordered.

His was clearly a liberating mission (Lk. 4:18–19). The liberation which he offered touched every aspect of man's existence in the world. First and foremost he challenged the prevailing world-view, based on the security of law (the ritual holiness of the Jews, and the law and order of the Romans). In place of the security of the law he offered the maturity of a love-relationship based on the acknowledgement and reality of sins forgiven (Lk. 7:40–50). Then, secondly, he challenged every kind of superhuman oppressive power, from whose control man could not free himself. These were the threatening forces of nature (Mk. 4:35–41), demon-possession (Mk. 5:1–20), physical disability (Mk. 5:25–34; Lk. 13:11–13) and greed (Lk. 19:1–10).

What Jesus never offered, however, was complete liberation in this present age from the complex of ambiguous political power.

[10] O. Cullmann, *Jesus and the Revolutionaries* (New York, 1970); M. Hengel, *Was Jesus a Revolutionist?* (Philadelphia, 1971); *Victory over Violence* (Philadelphia, 1973); S. G. F. Brandon, *Jesus and the Zealots* (Manchester, 1967); Yoder, *The Politics of Jesus* (Grand Rapids 1972).

[11] *Cf.* my article 'The Messianic Role of Jesus and the Temptation Narrative: a Contemporary Perspective', *EQ*, 44, 1972, 1, 2.

Such liberation belongs only to the time of the new creation of all things (Mt. 19:28).

Two alternative ways of achieving a dramatic political change were possible: the way of the Zealots, which would have established the upholders of moral self-righteousness in power (modern political revolutions are also based on the claim to a superior righteousness), or the way of subversion of the system from within by a new kind of society based on a new kind of power. The first way, the use of superior force, could have achieved sudden change; the second way, however, could only be gradual for it depended entirely upon the lengthy process of achieving harmony between means and ends.

Clearly Jesus' attitude towards liberation depended upon his diagnosis of man's oppression. By discovering the root cause within man himself (Mk. 7:20–23), he shows himself to be at one with the prophets. Social injustice springs from a variety of factors – lust for power, greed, hatred, insecurity – all of them part of the universal lie that man really is free when he challenges God and denies God's purpose for his creation (Jn. 8:31ff.; 18:36–19:16; Rom. 1:25). Only by repentance and conversion to the truth that God's purpose is achieved only through the way of Jesus can a new order of things possibly be established.[12]

So novel is Jesus' reaction to the questions of power and change that mankind as a whole has missed the fact that his acceptance of death at the hands of legalistic law-breakers is a truly revolutionary act. One of the main reasons why political revolutions are doomed to failure is that they have no means of exorcizing guilt. There is no way of being truly reconciled with former enemies, no way of expiating the death of the innocent, no way of measuring the balance and meaning of the suffering demanded. There is no forgiveness in revolutionary politics. So there can be no genuine liberation without a sin-bearer who takes upon himself the horror of the separation between God and man caused by guilt (Mk. 10:45; 15:34–35).

But death by itself is only a heroic gesture of self-sacrifice. If a real material resurrection of this same Jesus did not take place,

---

[12] On the question of repentance in the life of the nations, *cf.* the interesting article of A. Solzhenitsyn, 'Repentance and Self-Limitation in the Life of Nations' in A. Solzhenitsyn *et al.*, *From Under the Rubble* (London, 1975), pp. 105–143.

Schweitzer's thesis (followed in part by the Marxist Machovec[13]), that Jesus' apocalyptic expectation of the inauguration of a new age was frustrated, is the most valid one. Jesus, on this view, was a truly noble, but ultimately futile, revolutionary visionary. On this view, he started a movement for change which was intrinsically incapable of maintaining its impetus. And when revolutionary movements lose their thrust for genuine change they become disillusioned. Disillusionment leads to a growing divorce between revolutionary language and practice. The rapid descent to the impassioned defence of the mere form of revolution in a reactionary power structure is all the more dramatic by reason of the lofty height of rhetoric from which it has occurred.

The resurrection of Jesus is, then, the only door through which the power and reality of a new order can enter this world.

The early church

The revolutionary presence of Jesus in the new community he founded was not simply a memory, nor a repetition of revolutionary language and symbols, but an objective reality through the gift of the Holy Spirit. The resurrection of 'this same Jesus' meant that the disciples were already living the reality of the new age. The eschatological forces of God's Kingdom were already operating in the middle of time.

It is true that, before Pentecost, the disciples still held to the revolutionary expectations of the old age (Acts 1:6). They looked for independence, autonomy and the economic and political splendours of the kingdom of David and Solomon. The redemption of Israel (Lk. 2:38; 19:42; 24:21) meant the cultural and religious chauvinism of a particular people. And yet, who can deny that national pride has often been one of the strongest motivations for revolutionary change? What emerged at Pentecost, through the baptism of the Spirit, was a concept of revolution coming from the new age, a new universal theocracy.

From its very birth the church had to decide its racial policy (Acts 6:1ff.; 10.9ff.; 15:1ff.). The entry of the Gentiles into the new community on a completely equal footing with the Jews was, in

---

[13] Machovec, A Marxist looks at Jesus (London 1976).

itself, a revolution of incalculable consequences. It signifies a transcendence of narrow nationalist aspirations and demonstrated the power of Jesus' presence to produce a new motive to guide social relationships.

Paul, reflecting later in his life on the significance of Christ's death and resurrection for the elimination of relationships based on domination and exploitation (Gal. 3:25–29; Col. 3:9–11), says that this new community is at the very centre of God's purpose for humanity (Eph. 3:3–11).

In thinking about the revolutionary implications of the gospel the concept of the two ages seems to be at the heart of the early church's missionary thinking. The old age is characterized by the law of sin and death (Rom. 8:2), which manifests itself in *legal righteousness*, without genuine repentance and faith; in *human wisdom*, without knowledge of God's purposes; and in *political and economic power*, without compassion for the weak in society. Paul struggled against the first in Romans and Galatians, and against the second in First Corinthians. The third is found in the Letter of James and in John's vision of Babylon, the great harlot (Rev. 17–18).

The New Testament's revolutionary expectation, then, is concentrated in the new age leading to the new creation (Heb. 12:22–29; 2 Pet. 3:13; Rev. 21–22). It influences every ethical problem facing the church, from the authority of the state (Rom. 13:1–7; 1 Pet. 2:13–17) to its attitude towards the poor (1 Cor. 16:1–2; 2 Cor. 8–9; Gal. 2:10;), and makes radical demands for a wholly new life-style (Rom. 12:1–2, 9–21; Eph. 4:17–24).

Hope is not disappointed for it springs from a real, present experience of God's liberating and transforming power (Acts 4:30; 5:12; Heb. 2:4).

Chapter Ten

A question of method

The development of production and the acquisition of wealth have become the highest goals of the modern world. . . . This is the philosophy . . . which is now being challenged by events.
E. F. Schumacher, *Small is Beautiful* (1973).

Christians as well as humanists have bought into the religion of growth at a fearful cost – the loss of their own spiritual and prophetic traditions.
Robert L. Stivers, *The Sustainable Society* (1976).

Unless new forms of Christianity are allowed to emerge, encouraged to emerge, then throughout the world those who live in the secular city will be denied religion.
Alistair Kee, *The Scope of Political Theology* (1978).

Our survey is finished. We have seen how a small sample of theologians have personally encountered revolution. Can we draw any firm conclusions from our visit to different continents? Each of us will probably be struck by different aspects of the discussion. In this final chapter I shall venture a few of my own impressions.

As far as revolution is concerned, the initial impulse came from what we might term apocalyptic movements within Christianity. These were minority groups who became disenchanted with the power structures derived from the Constantinian union of church and state. Making a radical distinction between obedience to Christ and obedience to Caesar, they became the first non-conformists of the modern era. Some believed in a Zealot-type overthrow of the existing 'Babylon', while others organized themselves into separate societies, refusing allegiance to the state at certain crucial points such as military service and oath-taking.

The Reformation, though not mainly inspired by apocalyptic

visions of the new Jerusalem, produced a body of thought which hastened the dissolution of centuries of political and religious tradition. In particular, it undermined belief in the givenness and eternity of the existing order. The developed Constantinian model of society, known as caesaropapism (the union of throne and altar), so perfectly illustrated by the Spanish dynasty of the early 16th century, was challenged by a series of revolutionary changes in theological belief: personal faith in and accountability to Jesus Christ, leading to the absolute worth of each individual in the management of society; a desacramentalized church; the abandonment of natural law (what is eternal to the human system) as a basis for moral choice and direct application of biblical laws to the affairs of the state; the refusal to accept traditions, customs or authority which could not be defended on the basis of Scripture. Though not producing revolution in the strict sense, the Reformation did provoke a profound questioning of hitherto tacitly accepted values. When the basic world-view of a culture is challenged by one which proves itself to be superior, its institutions and values are bound to change as well.

First Deism and then 18th-century philosophical scepticism completed the demolition job. The divine right of kings was transformed into the divine right of the people. Decisions in society would no longer be taken on the basis of unquestioned authority; theoretically, the consensus of the 'majority' would prevail. In the revolutions of 1776 and 1789 the 'majority' were the burgeoning, creative, self-assured middle-classes. Their philosopher was Hegel and their prophet Adam Smith. They were confident of being the harbingers of a totally new order. From 1848 onwards the 'majority' were the proletariat, the only group in society who drew no benefits from the new, exploitative order of capitalism. The burning of their chains would signal the end of the oppressive state. Only then would the 'objective conditions' for a new order exist, in which 'the free development of each is the condition for the free development of all' (*Communist Manifesto*). Their philosopher and prophet was Marx.

But the new order has never been born, and the revolutionary movements have proved to be either sterile or abortive. There are undoubtedly many factors which account for their successive failures, but common to all is an inadequate understanding of man and his place in history. The Reformation doctrine of man's depravity

gave way two centuries later to Rousseau's doctrine of man's innocence: man was ill-educated, oppressed by superstitions and illusions; not fully developed; alienated by his conditions of work, but
never basically immoral.

When the revolutionaries began to speak about the agents of the
new order, they were constantly tripped up by their own optimism.
From Robespierre to Gutiérrez hope has been successively placed in
the people, the proletariat, the peasants, the industrial working class
and the Third World poor. They are the chosen race to be a light to
the nations and the basis of a new, fraternal, 'messianic' community.
But who has chosen them? History, thunders Marx; the God of the
exodus, reflects Gutiérrez. But, one suspects, they have really been
chosen by middle-class revolutionary theorists. In fact, they have
never been allowed to initiate change from their own perspective.
The revolutionary cadres have been too busy shouting orders to
listen to those who once again have been forced to suffer estrangement from decisions about their own future.

Revolutions have failed because they have accepted the theory of
human innocence. Their account of the world has been too simplis-
tic; it has uniformly ignored the complexities of human social life.
Claiming to be based on empirical investigation, it has walked blind-
fold into the brick wall of the facts it has ignored. For example, the
modern Marxist interpretation of political and economic processes,
because it is inflexible, authoritarian and reductionist, becomes more
dated each year. Today, I believe, a person can be a Marxist only on
ideological or psychological grounds, because he needs some kind
of coherent belief-system. Marxism no longer represents a revolutionary option.[1]

Underestimating the problem of man's inner alienation, all revolutions up to the present have been concerned only with the mechan-
ics of change. Socialism, for example, changes the ownership of the
means of production. What needs revolutionizing, however, are both
the means themselves and the ends on which they are based. What

[1] As Alexander Solzhenitsyn has often pointed out, not least in a lecture given at Harvard
University (May 1978), its essential materialism produces an ultimately static view of society. In
the face of failure there are no resources for renewal. It becomes bogged down in absurd
rationalizations. I have reviewed Miguez's assertion that Christians ought to aid Marxism to
recapture its spent revolutionary dynamic in 'Beyond Capitalism and Marxism: Dialogue with a
Dialogue' *Theological Fraternity Bulletin*, 1976, Nos.1–2, pp. 26ff.

difference does it make, for example, to the Two-Thirds world, who live outside all meaningful development processes, if capital and technology are owned by the state or by huge individual corporations? The development model on which both are based is not appropriate to their situation. So the One-Third world passes by on the other side (the capitalist priest and the socialist levite), because the wretched of the earth need food, clothing, adequate shelter, access to preventive medicine and education, not the inessential 'necessities' of the consumer society.[2]

And who has stopped to enquire what the means are supposed to produce, and why? Do we work to produce in order to consume? Or, do we work in order to display the rich variety of God's creation: man, an imaginative and inventive artist, in partnership with his creator discovering the creative possibilities of his world? There simply cannot be any genuine revolution until we have settled the issue of the meaning of change and brought together means and ends into a coherent whole.

Unfortunately, we are still dominated by the 18th-century model of progress. Our teachers are still Adam Smith and Karl Marx. We are devoid of sufficient creativity to devise a different model, and until we do it would clarify issues greatly if we were to call a moratorium on the use of the word revolution.

Nevertheless, we should recognize that the whole debate has done an immense service to contemporary theology. I cannot see how the practice of theology can remain the same for those who take seriously the questions and answers which revolutionary theory and practice have put to human life in the modern world. Let us try to spell out this challenge.

In the first place, and principally, it is clear that traditional theological methods have been quite unable to respond to the human challenge implicit in revolutionary thinking. Examples of this are the division of theology into self-contained areas of specialization, which has effectively divorced ethics, systematic theology and biblical studies, from each other, and an approach to the Bible which implies that it can be 'scientifically' studied without consideration of the interpreter's historical and cultural situation. This situation has ari-

[2] *Cf.* R. Sider, *Rich Christians in an Age of Hunger*, chapters 1 and 2.

sen, it would seem, mainly from the distance which the academic pursuit of theology maintains between its particular preoccupations and the human life-and-death struggles going on outside the ivory towers.[3] At the very best, such issues are relegated to the classroom where social ethics is taught, if indeed it is taught at all. The problem is well summed up by Avery Dulles:

> In many universities today, theology is fitted to a Procrustean bed of academic regulations that tend to blunt its impact as a *reflection on the commitment of faith*.[4]

In other words, theology in the Western world is captive to institutions, and not only universities, but seminaries and colleges as well.

So, in the second place, the greatest task confronting theology today is that of revising its methodology from top to bottom (or, perhaps, from bottom to top). The theologies we have been reviewing have made certain radical and uncompromising statements. Moltmann states that the proper context for theology is the local church.[5] Liberation Theology maintains that theology is Christian and biblical only when it starts by reflecting on the meaning of what is happening in the world, using to this end analytical tools developed by the social sciences. Cone says that Christian theology can be undertaken only from within a suffering community, and more particularly one suffering the evil effects of racism. Boesak argues that Black Theology must be a subversive theology whose principal task is to end white innocence concerning the real causes and effects of separate

---

[3] *Cf.* W. Wink, *The Bible in Human Transformation* (Philadelphia, 1976); P. Minear, 'Ecumenical Theology – Profession or Vocation?', *TT*, 32, 1976, pp. 66–73; and the debate on his article: 'Symposium on Biblical Criticism', *TT*, 33, 1977, pp. 354–367.

[4] 'Symposium on Biblical Criticism', p. 360 (my italics).

[5] *Cf. The Open Church: Invitation to a Messianic Life-Style* (London, 1978), pp. 9, 115. In an unpublished paper 'The Congregation of Christ and the Signs of the Spirit' (Buenos Aires, 1977), he states (p. 3): 'Diaconia, mission and ecumenism belong to the task of the congregation and ought not to be removed from it. Theology also belongs to it, and ought not to be withdrawn into seminaries and faculties. On the contrary, the congregation and its members ought not to be deprived any longer of its own mission, being replaced by professionals. We have delegated too many tasks to specialists. This is the reason why personal effort becomes atrophied. At the beginning it may seem a relief to the congregation to receive a pastor, deacon or informed spiritual guide; but this always ends in alienation.' (My translation from the Spanish.)

development. Lehmann's main thesis is that theology can help pre-serve revolutions from their own destruction, while, finally, Metz says that theology's principal task is to add its unique contribution to the shaping of tomorrow's world.

Though serious differences remain between some of these theologians,[6] they all believe that the key to an authentic Christian theology today is a relevant biblical hermeneutic. Brevard Childs sums up the crisis of traditional theology and points forward to a new era of theological activity:

> the historical critical method increasingly offers diminishing returns for a serious understanding of the Bible within the Church. The method . . . has (not) provided a link between the church and the world by which the gospel can be more effectively proclaimed.[7]

Theology, then, faces three crucial questions: *how, why* and *where* is the Bible being interpreted? Let us begin with the last question first. Probably the most penetrating criticism of contemporary academic theology comes from Third World Christian leaders. Segundo, for example, maintains that theology has fallen prey to the propaganda of the consumer society,[8] limiting its area of research to an intellectual study of historical documents without any corresponding application to those problems which the consumer society has itself been responsible for causing.

Western theology is captive to a long tradition of dialogue with changing philosophical systems;[9] it has been largely unresponsive to insights on human reality gleaned from the social sciences.

For Third World Christians only an 'engaged' theology is of any value, *i.e.* one which springs directly from the hopes, struggles, sorrows and guilt of real people in real situations. But theology can

---

[6] *Cf.* J. Moltmann, 'On Latin American Liberation Theology': an Open Letter to José Miguez Bonino', *Christianity and Crisis*, 36, 29 March 1976.

[7] 'Symposium on Biblical Criticism', *op. cit.*, p. 359.

[8] *Cf. Acción pastoral latinoamericano*, pp. 19–26.

[9] *Cf.* R. Taber, 'Is there More than One Way to Do Theology?' *Gospel in Context*, 1, 1978, pp. 5–6, for some of the reasons for this. Kwame Bediako argues: 'that the crucial question for Western theology is not whether it must persist in speaking in philosophical idiom, it is to discover whether the real life-issues of today in the West are being posed in philosophical terms and whether the challenges to the Gospel come from the philosophical schools.' *Ibid.*, p. 14.

engage with daily reality only if those who study it actually participate in the real life of ordinary people. Theology in the Bible and in
the early church was certainly the province of people who were
actively involved at the centre of God's plan of salvation for the
world.

The concrete situation will also inevitably determine the purpose
of theology. It is much easier for the institutional and unengaged
pursuit of theology to continue in situations of affluence and relative
stability. In the Western world, for some time yet, theology can be
pursued as an end in itself (though, sooner or later, an increasing
economic crisis will probably end its privileges). In the Third World,
it has continually to serve the task of God's people to make known
the gospel of the Kingdom for the poor. Theology's purpose, then
is to elucidate this task in particular circumstances. One chief aim of
its study of the Scriptures will be to purify all theology of extraneous
philosophical, ideological and cultural elements, inherited from the
West,[10] enabling it to apply fresh analysis to situations it has never
before encountered.

Finally, theology will follow the method of the hermeneutical
circle. It will search the Scriptures with questions arising out of the
church's specific evangelistic, prophetic and diaconic ministries, and
it will allow the original meaning of the text to challenge the idolatries
of power and the idolatries of privilege which so often shape the life
of both church and world. Theology, as in biblical times, will once
again be in the front line of protest against all alienated existence. At
the same time, it will show how life in the new age is applicable to
the way we shape our planet's future.

We agree with Childs that the study of the Scriptures must be 'de-
professionalized', so that God's people can see that it is a serious
task within their capabilities. Professional biblical scholars and
church leaders have 'tribalized' the Bible; it now needs to be univ
ersalized so that ordinary Christians can contribute their God-given
measure of spiritual wisdom.

Above all the Bible should be interpreted from the praxis of the
cross and resurrection by Christian disciples who are caught up in
the mystery of Christ's suffering and triumph in his world.

[10] Cf. Gospel and Culture: The Willowbank Report (Wheaton, 1978).

183

Index

185